AF538396

The Grand Lady of Fourth Avenue

Portland's Historic Multnomah Hotel

The Grand Lady of Fourth Avenue

Portland's Historic Multnomah Hotel

Cáit Curtin

Binford & Mort Publishing
Portland, Oregon

For

All my family, with love and thanks;
and

D. P. J.
the best of friends

The Grand Lady of Fourth Avenue
Portland's Historic Multnomah Hotel

Printed in the United States of America

Library of Congress Catalog Card Number: 97-74242
ISBN: 0-8323-0521-9

First Edition 1997

Contents

Foreword

A hotel very often can be a microcosm of the community in which it is a part: its staff reflects the degree of friendliness the community has for strangers; its kitchen serves samples of the local cuisine; its gift shop provides representative tokens of the city and region, and its newsstand provides up-to-the-minute political, social, and economic information about the citizens and their community. With just a mention of its name, such a hotel evokes the very essence of the city: Paris's *Ritz*; London's *Grosvenor*; Tokyo's *New World*; New York's *Plaza*, and San Francisco's *St. Francis*.

The Multnomah Hotel in Portland, Oregon, is such a place. For fifty years and more it provided thousands of visitors with a small piece of Portland and those thousands of visitors, in turn, carried away with them the beauty of the city and the gracious hospitality of its people to all parts of the world. For many, the Multnomah was their first and only experience of Portland, and one they never forgot. Others were so captivated by the place and surroundings that they returned again and again.

To become such a microcosm of a particular place, a hotel must become one with the city. It must host the city's major events, support its good works, and reflect its social customs. Most importantly, it must make itself inviting to the community, endearing itself to the people by welcoming them into its heart. Perhaps more than any other hotel in the city, the Multnomah Hotel did just that in Portland.

From its opening day, the Multnomah invited Portlanders in at every opportunity: on that day over eight thousand people visited the hotel, each individually greeted by the managing director. Each subsequent day of operation brought hundreds more through the Pine Street doors, drawn by the Multnomah's reputation for wonderful service and the city's best entertainment. From vaudeville to recitations, from operatic solos to ballroom dancing, from fine dining to western-theme grills, and for Christmas, Easter, and the Fourth of July, the Multnomah welcomed everyone from Portland's high society to the small child eager to meet Santa Claus at a holiday breakfast.

When Charles A. Lindbergh, the "Lone Eagle," visited Portland after his record-setting flight across the Atlantic, the Multnomah invited over a thousand of his admirers to a dinner in his honor. Likewise, when President Eisenhower visited, several hundred Republican supporters celebrated by lunching at the Multnomah. When Jimmy Stewart, Lana Turner, Bing Crosby and Bob Hope stayed at the Multnomah, their fans approached them with ease and sometimes shared a short conversation with them. Before World War II, would-be Fred Astairs and Ginger Rogers could enter the Multnomah's grand ballroom in their imagination and dance to the music of the hotel's orchestra in their own living rooms via radio station KXL's live broadcast of the Sunday night entertainment.

Generations of Portlanders grew to love the Multnomah because of its welcoming friendliness. A special few loved it even more because it was, truly, part of themselves.

This story about the Multnomah Hotel is a story about people–people who came from far away places and people who came every Sunday for lunch after church. But the people most important to this story are those who worked at the Multnomah, who polished its floors, scrubbed its bathrooms, cooked its food, and treated its guests with the same courtesy and helpfulness they treated each other. Many of the Multnomah's staff regarded their work at the hotel as more than just a job. Whether bellman, cook, maid or manager, they considered themselves personally responsible for providing each guest and visitor with a unique experience. The Multnomah's popularity reflected their dedication, and this popularity fostered an increasing pride and desire among the staff to do their best each day. The success of their effort is apparent: for the past thirty-two years the Multnomah Hotel has remained alive in the memories of Portlanders even when it no longer welcomed the legions of visitors it once did.

So it is not so surprising that the Multnomah will once again open its doors to guests. In 1995, the Embassy Suites, a leading national hotel chain known for its attention to the comfort of its patrons, seized what its owners felt to be a grand opportunity to revive the Multnomah and renew its close relationship with the City of Portland. Buying the hotel, which had stood empty since 1991 when the government offices moved out, the company made plans to turn it into a premier property while at the same time preserving its classic beauty. To that end, the lobby and mezzanine as well as the exterior of the building have been placed on the National Register of Historic Places.

Because of their care, the Multnomah Hotel has again opened its doors to strangers, soon to make them old friends as it did before. And as before, it will be the people—staff, Portlanders and guests—who will again make a place in the heart of Portland for the "Grand Lady of Fourth Avenue."

Acknowledgements

The following individuals and institutions were indispensable to telling the story of the Multnomah Hotel. While I give them all credit for their invaluable contributions, I take full responsibility for any errors found within.

Paul Christensen, for wanting to find the story behind the beautiful building he bought and the wisdom to add another chapter to that story by inviting Embassy Suites to make the Multnomah once again Portland's most magnificent hotel.

Those former Multnomah Hotel employees, for their love and devotion to the "Grand Lady" and for never letting her pass beyond their memories, especially:

Bill Keithan, whose foresight contributed to a store of knowledge about the Multnomah Hotel and Western Hotels Inc.

Gordon Bass (deceased), who on his eighty-sixth birthday could vividly recall his first job for WHI at the Multnomah Hotel in 1935 and provided critical information about the company.

Hal Carey, Bill Williams, Jim Gimarelli, and Clauzelle Fox for their intimate and detailed knowledge of the hotel, its guests, and its employees.

P. K. Wall, who provided valuable information about her father, Bob Kennedy, and the Multnomah's publicity campaigns.

Mulla Hauser Myers, *Anne Hauser Sola, and Norma Faricy Condee*, granddaughters of Eric V. Hauser, Sr., whose personal reminiscences of their grandfather and family filled in many of the details about the Multnomah in the years 1916 until it closed in 1965.

Hugh Ackroyd, Portland photographer *par excellence* and crony of many of the Multnomah's managers, for relating many of the wild times he and they had.

Walt Gadsby, who remembered the lovely "Bundles for Britain" story.

Colleen Schafroth, curator of education, Maryhill Museum of Art, who added greatly to the stories of Sam Hill and Queen Marie.

Carol Lichtenberg, photo archivist, Washington State University, Pullman, for allowing access to the WHI and Multnomah photos and artifacts.

Kris A. White, manuscripts librarian/archivist and *the staff of the Oregon Historical Society*, for their patience and their helpfulness.

Ray Watson, senior vice president and division general manager, KXL Radio, for allowing access to KXL's photo and newsclip archives.

Ralph Nelson, Oregon Symphony Association, for information on the symphony galas held at the Multnomah.

Margaret Barss, who has always been my model and inspiration, and without whose skillful editing this manuscript would be one long, run-on sentence.

Pam Henningsen, Binford & Mort, for being flexible enough to turn the publishing process upside down in order to bring this book to press.

And to all those Portlanders who called and wrote to tell their stories of the Multnomah Hotel.

Because they never forgot, the "Grand Lady" lives on.

Announcement

The Management of the

Hotel Multnomah

"The Most Magnificent Hostelry in the Northwest"

Opening Tomorrow, Feb. Eighth

Offers a Limited Number of Rooms and Suites to Permanent Guests at Exceptional Rate Inducements

The Management has reserved a number of choice rooms and suites for rental to permanent guests. To those who desire to make the Multnomah their home exceptionally moderate rates will be made.

The people who want the best there is will find in the Multnomah every comfort, every convenience attainable in a hotel of the size, magnificence and palatial appointments of this—the finest and best in the Northwest.

The structure, built and equipped at an expense of over Two Million Dollars, is absolutely fireproof. Every room is an outside room, assuring a constant abundance of light and air. Of the 725 rooms and suites, 300 have a private bath.

The superb lobby, the writing rooms, the parlors, the restaurants, the service—all are at disposal of the guest, whether permanent or transient.

Detailed floor plans and Rates will be furnished on application

Multnomah Hotel Company

H. C. Bowers
Manager

J. M. Brownell
Assistant Manager

The Oregonian

Multnomah Hotel Company announces the opening of "The Most Magnificent Hostelry in the Northwest"

Portland, Oregon woke up to a cold, blustery morning on Wednesday, February 7, 1912. The headline story in *The Morning Oregonian* announced "Washington's Eye is Upon Orozco," and informed Portlanders that President Taft and his cabinet were seriously concerned that a renegade Mexican general might provoke a fight for secession in the State of Chihuahua which bordered on Texas. The president's concern was great enough to order all western army posts to stand at ready alert.

Closer to home, the United Improvement Clubs Association, a group of local businessmen, adopted a resolution approving an interstate bridge across the Columbia River to Vancouver, Washington, after hearing a report by J.H. Nolta of the Columbia River Bridge Committee; a burglar was frightened away by the crying of a baby he had disturbed when entering a home on northeast Union Avenue, and sales of postage stamps at the main post office amounted to $6900, the largest one-day total ever. The weather was to remain typically cold, windy, and rainy. And prominent on page seven was a full-page announcement that the "Most Magnificent Hostelry in the Northwest" would be offering a "limited number of rooms and suites to permanent guests at exceptional rate inducements."

Having only time enough to read the paper's front page and look for the advertisement announcing the opening of his new hotel, Philip Gevurtz rushed to arrive downtown by 7:00 o'clock that morning. The next day, he was scheduled to open the front door of the two million dollar, nine-story, 700-room hotel he had named the Multnomah. Begun in 1910, the building was the largest (but not the tallest) structure in Portland. Located at 4th Avenue and Pine Street on the edge of the business district of the fast-growing city, the Multnomah occupied the entire block, one of only a few buildings to do so.

The next morning, February 8, Gevurtz had no time to peruse his morning paper. Opening day promised to be hectic and he wanted the ceremonies to begin on time. Before sitting down to the first breakfast (for 600) the hotel would serve later that day, Gevurtz, accompanied by a party of dignitaries, rode the elevator to the roof, tied a golden key to a bunch of balloons, and sent it soaring into the gray cloudiness of Portland's winter sky. No one knows how far that golden key traveled, but for the next 53 years, the Multnomah Hotel played host to the famous, the powerful, and those ordinary men and women conventioneers who represented hundreds of American business and professional organizations. During the course of a long life, the Multnomah Hotel would gather in all of Portland through its double doors, welcoming generations of Portlanders with its gracious hospitality, and marking the city's memorable events with its unequaled warmth and friendliness, to become, truly, the "Grand Lady of Fourth Avenue."

Oregon Historical Society Negative Number OrHi 93287

Early Hotel Multnomah brochures featured these likenesses of Native American Indians from the Multnomah tribe, a local tribe of the Wappatos (Chinooks). Later, the hotel's new owners dropped the braves from the Multnomah logo and advertisements.

Courtesy of Washington State University

The Multnomah Hotel–1919

ONE MAN'S DREAM

Early Days of the Multnomah Hotel

By 1910, Portland, Oregon was a growing town, made accessible and popular by its situation as the hub of shipping and industry on the Columbia River. Only fifty-three years after attaining statehood, Oregon was already attracting individuals from all over the United States and Canada, people eager to make their fortune in its largest city, Portland, early dubbed the "River City." The resulting population boom in Portland soon convinced the city fathers of a need for a plan to control growth.

A major player in the early development of the city was Philip Gevurtz, president of the Carlton and Multnomah Hotel Companies. Phil was a son of a Russian immigrant, Isaac Gevurtz, who, with his brother, had founded one of Portland's first furniture stores. Several years earlier, Phil had persuaded his father and uncle that Portland's growth offered an unprecedented opportunity to expand the family business to include furnishings for hotels and office buildings. The resulting financial windfall enabled Phil to buy into several promising hotel projects. Emboldened by their success, Phil decided to develop a hotel project of his own, the Carlton, and then another soon after when the block between

Courtesy of Washington State University

Construction of the Multnomah Hotel took over one year to complete and cost almost two million dollars. The photo above was taken November 3, 1910.

Courtesy of Washington State University

Thirteen months later, on December 14, 1911, the exterior was complete.

Southwest Third and Fourth Avenues and Pine and Oak Streets became available.

Knowing he was going to use the entire block, Gevurtz envisioned a hotel to rival those in the large western cities he had visited. Accustomed to traveling by train to San Francisco, Gevurtz and his wife had seen for themselves what luxuries a first-class hotel could offer the tired traveler. The firm of Gibson and Cahill was engaged to design the hotel and plans submitted to Gevurtz showed a classically detailed American Renaissance style building. Late in 1910, construction was begun and for the next twelve months work on the rising Multnomah Hotel proceeded.

Named after the local tribe of the Wappatos (Chinooks), the Multnomah would be the second largest hostelry in the Pacific Northwest, second only to the Olympic in Seattle. Covering the entire square block adjacent to Burnside Street, Portland's main, east-west thoroughfare, the Multnomah was soon to become the largest hotel in Portland, larger even than the city's famed Portland Hotel. From the beginning, its founder wanted the hotel to become an integral part of Portland society. During construction, he actively courted the local community and promised that the hotel would be available for civic activities and public use.

The Multnomah took over a year to construct, and cost almost two million dollars ($40 million in 1997 dollars). Its eight floors and lobby were designed to be free-standing, supported at each corner by pillars, leaving the interiors devoted entirely to usable space. Gevurtz wanted the hotel to attract a variety of customers: first and foremost conventioneers, then travelers wanting just a room for the night, as well as those requiring a two- or three-room suite for a lengthy visit in Portland, and those who would call the hotel "home" as permanent residents. So, along with traditional rooms and suites, the final design of over 700 rooms included one-room weekly rentals which shared bath and toilet facilities down the hall. At three dollars and fifty cents per week, these rooms were especially popular with railroad men because of their proximity to the Union Station. Permanent residents leased suites or rooms having their own baths and toilets.

Oregon Historical Society Negative Number OrHi 93288

An early Hotel Multnomah brochure featuring the lobby pillars and room rates
The lobby ceiling, ecru paint over plaster, is highlighted with 24K gilt.

© *Curt Teich Postcard Archives, Lake County (IL) Museum*

A view of the lobby and registration desk.

© *Curt Teich Postcard Archives, Lake County (IL) Museum*

Although this advertisement/postcard shows the Multnomah's impressive electric capabilities, it is unlikely that lights were hung around the top edges of the building wings.

On the seventh floor, the entire east wing contained rooms that could open up into each other via connecting doors. These Sample Rooms, two-room suites with bath, provided traveling salesmen with space to display their goods and entertain clients. They remained popular for years, especially with garment-industry reps from the east coast, California, and Seattle. Through the years, renovations improved and reconfigured the room layouts, but always on the seventh floor, there were suites that connected into each other.

On all floors, the corner rooms were the largest and most lavishly furnished. They had their own bathrooms with the finest of terrazzo flooring and claw-footed tubs. Traditionally, the largest room on the 8th floor was known as the Governor's Suite and included its own kitchen. As time went on, other rooms were designated in honor of some of the more prestigious Portland visitors. When Queen Marie of Romania came in 1926, she was housed in what came to be called the Queen's Suite on the second floor. Three connecting rooms on the seventh floor (770, 771, 772) were redecorated and furnished for President Eisenhower who visited thirty years later. From that time on, these rooms were always known as the Presidential Suite.

As important as these special guest suites were to the hotel's success, Gevurtz insisted that the Multnomah's public rooms be equally lavish and inviting so that the hotel would draw the large conventions that railroad travel to the Northwest was making possible. To attract this clientele, as well as to make the hotel a regular meeting-place for Portland's many clubs and activities, Gevurtz designed a magnificent lobby and mezzanine floor. The lobby featured a marble staircase, crystal chandeliers, and reflected lights salvaged from the Auditorium Hotel in Chicago. Twenty-four marble and terra cotta columns graced the room and supported the gilt ceiling. Beautiful high-backed mahogany chairs upholstered in a soft brown fabric and decorated with the Multnomah Hotel crest in yellow, matching sofas, and end tables provided luxurious lounging areas for patrons. Bellmen stood at attention at each column and were called to assist with guests and their luggage. They would move from column to column, nearer and nearer to the front desk as they were called. David Zaik, the hotel's first page boy, roamed the lobby, mezzanine and lower level, making announcements and paging guests.

Even more astutely, Gevurtz instructed the architect to design a special room on the lower level. The Arcadian Garden, "the most beautiful public room in the City," included a stage for the hotel's orchestra and a dining salon that could seat 600 people for dinner. This delightful room was decorated with scenic murals of the Pacific Northwest and featured a Pompeiian fountain in the center. The site of the first cabaret and vaudeville entertainment held in Portland, it also became a favorite choice for wedding receptions and other special occasions. The first wedding reception, held on Sunday, February 11, 1912, celebrated the marriage of Phil's daughter, Lillian.

From the lobby, the imposing staircase led to the mezzanine where nine banquet halls and meeting rooms were arranged. The grand ballroom was surrounded by three smaller banquet rooms opening on to it which, when opened, could seat 1200 guests. A full kitchen was located here. Together, the banquet rooms, the two lobby dining rooms, and grills could serve 2500 people at once.

However beautiful the Arcadian Garden and the lobby were, they were topped by the hotel's featured room, the Japanese Tea Room on the mezzanine. The only room in the hotel and one of the only places in Portland where women could smoke cigarettes in public without penalty, the Japanese Tea Room soon became a favorite of Portland's society matrons who liked to gather for luncheons and to examine the latest in fashions presented by Lipman Wolfe, one of Portland's leading department stores.

Other public rooms included a family grille on the main floor decorated in gray and blue, which seated 250-300 people and featured a homey, family-style atmosphere.

© Curt Teich Postcard Archives, Lake County (IL) Museum

Bellmen had regular stations at specific columns and as they were needed, they moved nearer and nearer to the front desk. The doors seen on the mezzanine opened into the banquet and ballrooms.

©Curt Teich Postcard Archives, Lake County (IL) Museum

The Multnomah Hotel crest decorated the high-backed mahogany chairs which provided luxurious seating.

Despite being windowless because of its location on the lower level, the Arcadian Garden featured natural greenery and folliage.

At various times the fountain in the Arcadian Garden was described as "Neapolitan" or "Pompeiian."

OPENING DAY—FEBRUARY 8, 1912

By June 3, 1911, construction had reached the top story, and advertising in the *Hotel News* trade paper made much of the fact that 180 rooms had hot and cold running water and 300 actually had baths. I. Gevurtz and Sons were to provide much of the furnishings for the hotel. Gevurtz recruited H.C. Bowers, part owner of The Bowers Hotel, to manage the Multnomah. Bowers signed a 10-year contract at $10,000 yearly salary, and soon sold his interest in The Bowers to Mr. Williams of Salem for $20,000.

Besides Bowers, the 300-member staff included such leaders as: Julian Brownell, assistant manager, formerly assistant manager of the Palace Hotel in San Francisco; Emil Gigoux, head chef, from the Waldorf Astoria in New York, who, as part of his five-year contract with the Multnomah Hotel Company, brought his entire kitchen staff, including the pastry chef with him. W. B. Martlin, the maitre d'hôte, came from the Knickerbocker in New York City; Clyde McAtee, the head steward, from New York's famous Sherry Hotel, and A. R. Edwards, the wine steward, from the Congress Hotel in Chicago.

Finally, only thirty days past the originally scheduled opening date, the Multnomah Hotel opened on Thursday, February 8, 1912. The night before, a dinner was served to members of the press, and as the *Hotel News* reported, representative members of Portland's news agencies were present, as well as many others from Seattle and San Francisco and points in between. Subsequent complimentary stories run by *The Oregonian* and other local and regional papers about the hotel and Gevurtz indicate that from the very beginning, the Multnomah knew that favorable publicity was the path to success.

Beginning with the key ceremony and breakfast,

Oregon Historical Society Negative Number Or Hi 26681

Chief Multnomah provides an impressive focal point to the advertisement of the beautiful Multnomah Hotel (note the name change from Hotel Multnomah).

festivities continued throughout opening day, during which more than 8,000 people toured the new hotel. So many of Portland's business and social elite had made reservations for dinner the first night that celebratory "first" dinners had to be stretched out during the entire week in order to accommodate all who wanted to dine at the new establishment.

Invited guests at the first night's banquet included members of the Portland Commercial Club, the Chamber and Junior Chamber of Commerce, and the Manufacturers Association. Prominent Portland businessmen, H.L. Pittock, Theodore S. Wilcox, and Charles J. Henry were the featured speakers.

Appropriately enough, the celebrations ended later that month on February 29, when Mayor Rushlight proclaimed the day, "Greater Portland Day," to celebrate the city's plan to adopt a "Portland Plan of Growth and Development," the first such plan to be formulated for the fast-growing city. The Chamber of Commerce sponsored a grand dinner at the city's most glittering representative of the growth it had so recently experienced, the Multnomah Hotel. Already the hotel was making its mark as a gathering place for the city's civic leaders.

EARLY MARKETING EFFORTS

Even before opening day, the hotel had booked its first convention. The International Brotherhood of Elks chose it to be the headquarters of their annual convention in July. The Elks were delighted that the Multnomah could accommodate their entire convention for meetings and banquets, even though not all the 1500 or more delegates could be housed there. (The nearby Portland Hotel accommodated the others.) From that time on during her long history, the Multnomah seldom saw a month that did not include at least one convention.

The first Multnomah Publicity Manager, Monroe "Goldie" Goldstein was a bright, young man who had a knack for attracting business. With Phil Peltz, the hotel's first musical director, he arranged a full program of musical events for Portland's citizens and hotel guests, including free orchestral concerts every Sunday evening in the lobby. By October, the hotel was hosting complementary recitals on the first Saturday of each month. One of the first artists was Ellen Beach Young, a lyric soprano of worldwide fame.

Every afternoon from 3:30 to 5:00 p.m., the DeLory Trio played in the Japanese Tea Room. Between musical numbers, M. DeLory, a French scholar and writer, gave talks and recitations and conversed in French with attendees who could speak his language.

Along with booking conventions, Goldstein and other managers began a tradition which helped to secure the Multnomah's place in Portland's civic affairs. Hotel personnel became members of the various civic and social clubs in Portland and recruited these organizations to hold meetings and entertainment at the Multnomah. From its first days, the Multnomah hosted the Portland Adver-

Courtesy of the June Parker Matlock Collection

Parker Twins Dancers about 1940
One of the caberet acts which entertained at the Multnomah Hotel

MULTNOMAH HOTEL

THE MULTNOMAH, one of the largest hotels in the Northwest, occupies an entire city block and is located in the heart of the business section of Portland at 4th and Pine Sts. Because of its architectural beauty and interior grandeur, it has been termed by tourists, "*Their Western Home.*" The hotel is strictly fire-proof and modern in every detail. With 550 outside rooms, 350 with bath and many others en suite, the incoming guest is assured of accommodations that are both ample and pleasing to the most fastidious. The rooms are large, cozy and elegantly furnished and are given scrupulous care by competent maids.

LANE-MILES STANDISH CO.

Oregon Historical Society Negative Number MSS 1510

tising Club for its monthly luncheons, a tradition that lasted until the hotel closed in 1965. Other organizations and societies which met at the Multnomah included the Chamber of Commerce, the Propeller Club, the Knights of Columbus, the Elks Club, the Portland Rose Festival Association, and many others.

Goldstein and his successors traveled throughout the mid-west and east to publicize the hotel. In October 1912, during a 25-city tour of the east, Goldstein found that the fame of the Multnomah had often preceded him. On that tour, he arranged for the Army's Joint Chief of Staff, General Leonard Wood, and his traveling party to stay a week at the Multnomah while they were on official army business in the Northwest.

The Multnomah staff made it a priority to expedite reservations and transportation to the hotel upon arrival in Portland. Complementary hotel jitneys met every train and steamer and brought guests to the hotel. A guest could wire the hotel collect to make reservations for a future stay. Cards were kept on file regarding guests' likes and dislikes so when they returned, the staff could cater to their preferences.

Ease of making reservations was one thing, but Goldstein hatched even more exciting ideas of drawing visitors to Portland and the Multnomah. Perhaps his wildest brain-storm was to allow local dare-devil and stunt pilot, Silas Christofferson, to launch his single-engine Curtiss Pusher bi-plane from the roof of the Multnomah to make the first flight across the Columbia River to Vancouver, Washington. With much fanfare and publicity, a launch ramp was constructed, dignitaries were invited, and the date was set for June 13, 1912. The day dawned overcast, but the weather held, and Christofferson made a successful take-off and flight amid much cheering from the crowds lining the

Oregon Historical Society Negative Number Or Hi 24287

Dare-devil pilot, Silas Christofferson, ready for take-off from the roof of the Multnomah Hotel, June 13, 1912. Christofferson was just 22 years old when he made this historic flight. He went on to design and build planes in California, but was killed there four years later while testing a new proto-type plane.

Oregon Historical Society

View of the take-off from the roof of the Multnomah Hotel.

Oregon Historical Society Negative Number OrHi 24278-a

Bi-plane low over the city as Silas Christofferson takes off from the roof of the Multnomah Hotel.

streets around the hotel and from those waiting at the field (Pearson) in Vancouver. With him, he carried mail from Portland to Vancouver, some of the earliest "air mail" ever delivered. This singular, exciting event made an indelible impression on the Portland community and helped to establish the Multnomah's reputation as a modern, fun-loving, and congenial experience for hotel patrons and visitors to Portland alike.

THE DREAM DIES

Despite the success of Goldstein's marketing activities, Gevurtz was not realizing the return on his investment in the Multnomah Hotel that he had hoped for. In early 1912, soon after the Multnomah's opening, he had leased a building on the east side of the Willamette River at East Belmont Street and Grand Avenue, which he intended to use as a hotel that would be furnished by his newly reincorporated Gevurtz Furniture and Hotel Supply Company. Later that year, he also announced plans for another new hotel, the Vendome, at Northwest 20th and Everett Streets, at a cost of $275,000.

Unfortunately, Gevurtz had overextended himself. In addition to his investment in the Multnomah, Carlton, and Vendome Hotels, he had a financial interest in a dozen others that required ongoing investments of capital. The newly installed electric light plant in the Multnomah, which gave the hotel a 300 kilowatt electrical capacity at a cost of $1,000 each month for the light bill, plus the remodeling of the hotel's laundry, added to his financial plight. These and other expenditures outpaced revenues, and by January, 1913, Gevurtz was no longer able to operate the Multnomah at a profit. Portland's general economic downturn (actually a depression) also impacted Gevurtz's finances, so that in early 1913, less than a year after the opening of the Multnomah, He declared bankruptcy, citing the Multnomah Hotel Company's principal assets as $250,000 worth of furniture and fixtures.

Deciding to "concentrate his business efforts on his furniture stores and other properties," Gevurtz ceased operating the hotel on January 11, 1913. By coincidence, the estate of a former Portland businessman, R. R. Thompson, was looking for a smart investment. Its agent, Roy O. Yates, a San Francisco capitalist and business associate of Gevurtz, headed a San Francisco syndicate to purchase the Multnomah Hotel for the Thompson estate at a cost of $500,000. Yates then formed a new Multnomah Hotel Company to manage and operate the hotel, which he leased from the Thompson estate for $6,000 a month.

THE NEW MULTNOMAH HOTEL COMPANY

Yates retained General Manager Bowers as well as most of the staff. He immediately made some renovations such as decreasing the number of rooms to a more manageable 500 and putting an end to the nightly vaudeville shows in the Arcadian Garden. These shows, promoted by Bowers and Goldstein, were the first vaudeville shows held in Portland, but despite their popularity, they were expensive to produce. Yates estimated that it cost $500 a week to pay the actors and musicians. Not only was the $45,000 total cost to produce the shows exorbitant, he declared, he voiced his opinion that "this is not suitable entertainment for Portland . . ." and opted for lectures and the "more suitable" dinner music, featuring Herman Kenin's orchestra.

Yates built a marquee over the main entrance on Pine Street and extended it the full length of the building. He installed arc lights on the upper cornices for night-time illumination and replaced the public lavatories in the lobby. These renovations were completed just in time to accommodate Sarah Bernhardt when she entertained in Portland.

For the first anniversary of the hotel in February, 1913, Yates, Bowers, and "Goldie" Goldstein arranged a whole week of public celebration and entertainment. A band played every afternoon in the lobby, and the hotel's orchestra played dance music every evening in the ballroom. Local singers were invited to perform, and buffet luncheons were served, with Portland club members given special luncheon rates. The entire hotel was decorated with evergreens and bows highlighted by hidden electric globes for added beauty. The festivities and decorations continued during the visit of Miles

© *Curt Teich Postcard Archives, Lake County (IL) Museum*

Renovations to the Multnomah included the marquee over the Pine Street entrance and the arc lights on the upper cornices for night-time illumination

C. Moore, the former governor of Washington state, and of John L. Sullivan, the famous prize fighter who stayed several days at the Multnomah that winter.

YATES' FAILURE

Yates, unfortunately, was also unable to make the Multnomah pay financially. In 1916, complaining that he "had lost over $300,000 of his own money over the past three years," he, too, declared bankruptcy. Yates attributed the hotel's closing to Portland's general business depression and "apparent apathy of Portlanders to the hotel." He also noted that after Oregon had voted dry in October, 1914, bar receipts dropped off, and the hotel lost a significant portion of revenue. One newspaper at the time commented on the void the closure of the hotel would leave in Portland, but no one stepped forward to keep the Multnomah open and it appeared that the hotel's days would end after the last convention, the Riggs-Covey automobile show, which closed January 28, 1916. Sadly, Yates had the Multnomah boarded up and it sat empty for nine long months. Then another entrepreneur, realizing its potential, began an association that would lead to the Multnomah's growing reputation around the world and to the growth of a small hotel management company that would become a powerful player in the international hotel business.

Hauser Family Collection

Kenneth Hauser posing in front of his father, Eric V. Hauser Sr.'s portrait

ERIC V. HAUSER— HOTEL MAN

Before the 20th century was ten years old, Minnesotan Eric V. Hauser had begun to plan a rosy future for himself and his three sons–Rupert, Kenneth, and Eric Jr. These plans included traveling west to take advantage of the booming economic development that was flourishing all along the Pacific Northwest.

Born in 1865, in St. Paul, only eight years after Oregon had won statehood, Hauser exemplified the kind of self-made entrepreneur who was attracted by the opportunities held out by the young state to those willing to take chances and work hard. In 1885, after brief stints in Minneapolis as a printer's devil, newsboy, and compositor for several daily newspapers, the 20-year-old Hauser, with an eye for construction and a hunch that railroad service had a rich growth potential, returned to St. Paul to work for the Great Northern Railroad, initially as a dining room waiter, then as a construction worker.

Construction soon became his passion and a series of fortuitous associations helped him to move beyond a skilled railroad construction hand to a construction manager, and then general manager of some of Great Northern's large construction projects.

Great Northern's chairman and one of the country's

major railroad tycoons, James J. Hill, became Hauser's friend. When Hill told Hauser of his plans for establishing a railroad in the Pacific Northwest, Hauser, by then a member of Grant South Company, a well-known railroad construction firm, immediately found the opening he needed to realize his early dream. In 1907, he came to Portland where he met Sam Hill, another Minnesota native who had agreed with James J. Hill, his father-in-law, to build a railroad linking Washington and Oregon. The two Hills, with Grant South Co. and Hauser, took three years (1907-1909) to build the Spokane, Portland and Seattle Railway (SP&S). Those three years forged the early business relationship among Sam and James J. Hill and Eric Hauser into a deep and lasting friendship.

Returning to St. Paul, Hauser rejoined his wife, Nellie Anita Mason Hauser, whom he had married in 1884. The couple had four children–Rupert, Kenneth, Eric V. Jr., and Norma, the apple of her father's eye. Hauser bought a great mansion in St. Paul, where his wife and children lived while he traveled the country, constructing railroads and, eventually establishing his own company. Hauser Construction Company undertook several major projects such as building oil storage tanks in Honolulu for the Pan-Americal Oil Company and other more complicated engineering projects around the country.

After his experience with the Hills and the SP&S, Hauser began visiting the Pacific Northwest more frequently. More and more railroads were being constructed, and Sam Hill had sold Hauser on his dream of building roads in Oregon and Washington, especially along both sides of the Columbia River. Vast wheat farms in eastern Washington and Oregon and fruit orchards in the valleys east and west of the Cascade Mountains needed to be linked with the Port of Portland and eastern markets. At the same time, Hill knew that sooner rather than later the growing popularity and use of the automobile would make transportation of agricultural products much quicker and more convenient than by railroad. Without any lessening of his love for, and work in, building railroads, Sam Hill was also looking further and further ahead to the opening of the Pacific Northwest to commerce. Hauser, too, could see the possibilities, and eagerly accepted construction commissions from Sam Hill as well as contracts from Great Northern to extend the Oregon Trunk Railroad in central and eastern Oregon and the Southern Pacific's tunnel at Elk Rock, near Lake Oswego.

Hauser Settles in Portland

By the early teens, Eric Hauser, Sr. had moved permanently to Portland. Like Sam Hill's wife, Nellie Mason Hauser preferred to remain in St. Paul, except for occasional visits to Portland, and kept young Norma with her. As Rupert, Kenneth, and Eric Jr. became adults, they began working in their father's construction firm and then joined him in Portland.

During World War I, Hauser built ships for the U.S. Navy, and began a life of philanthropy by turning over his ship-building profits to the Red Cross and the Salvation Army as his way of contributing to the war effort. In 1924, he founded the Printer's Relief Fund, donating $1,000 as start-up money to establish a typographical union in Minneapolis, the scene of his first jobs in printing.

It was Eric, Jr. who, in 1916, brought the boarded-up Multnomah Hotel to his father's attention. During the previous January, the junior Hauser explained, the Multnomah Hotel Company had gone out of business and the Thompson estate had done nothing about finding a buyer for the place. Garnering information about the hotel from his Portland business associates and friends, Hauser began to see the possibilities of reopening the Multnomah, reputed to be one of the city's leading hotels, second only to the venerable Portland.

In deciding to buy the Multnomah, Hauser felt he could fulfill a long-time dream: to become a leading citizen and a respected member of the community. Through his business activities, he had become rich, and his philanthropic efforts had enhanced his respectability. Now he realized that owning and operating a magnificent hotel like the Multnomah would enable him to become a central figure in his adopted community and to complete the last phase of his life-long dream.

Hauser's ownership of the Multnomah gave him both a reason and an opportunity to play a prominent role in Portland's civic affairs. A stern, rather

PORTLAND, OREGON

THE MULTNOMAH HOTEL is at the cross roads of the Pacific Northwest—where rail meets trail, and all of the scenic grandeur of the old territory of the Hudson Bay Company becomes comfortably available to the traveler. The hotel is the "answer" to all inquiries as to whether the Northwest is civilized. The Multnomah is "Farthest West" of all great American hotels. Its cuisine is unsurpassed; its garage is a convenience to autoists, and its welcome is as cordial as the Northwest is wonderful.

Courtesy of the Oregon Historical Society

Multnomah Hotel ad circa 1920

gruff man, according to his granddaughter, Norma Condee, he seemed not to fit the persona of a genial, welcoming host and proprietor. But he was respected and well-liked by his fellow business associates for his honesty and industry. Finally, his long friendship with Great Northern officials and the irresistible Sam Hill enabled him to meet and entertain many prominent visitors to Portland during his thirteen-year ownership of the hotel.

Re-Opening the Multnomah

Hauser set October 10, 1916, as the date to reopen the Multnomah Hotel under his leadership. Before opening, however, he authorized a complete remodeling of the building, much of its beauty having been tarnished by so many months of neglect. The entire building was repainted, and all interior decorations were embellished. All panels and friezes in the lobby were painted in softer colors, and new furnishings were installed. The original high-backed lobby chairs were re-covered in fabric to match the new color scheme. Huge palms, ferns, and greenery were placed throughout the hotel, giving the public rooms a softer, more welcoming ambiance. A hotel and dining room silver service set, enough for very large parties, was ordered, and the hotel's 560 guest rooms were refitted with new furniture and carpets.

Hauser announced that a new manager, Harry E. Stinson, formerly of the Hotel Washington in Seattle, would handle the day-to-day operations of the hotel. Many former employees returned, and soon the full complement of 300 was reached.

The October 10 opening-day events included dinner parties in the Arcadian Garden, the lovely lower-level dining room, and a 7:30 p.m. banquet sponsored by the Women's Party for Inez Milholland Boissevain, a women's rights activist who was in Portland on a lecture tour. Three orchestras, including the hotel's, furnished music for the evening's celebrations, and a public dance was held in the grand ballroom, with music by the Gul Reazee Grotto.

The Multnomah Builds Its Reputation

Eric Hauser may not have been the most congenial host, but he definitely had a standard according to which he expected the hotel to operate. In this he had the full cooperation of his new manager, Harry Stinson. Whether because Stinson had perfected his skills at the famous Hotel Washington, or simply because of his personality, or possibly both, Stinson was able to discern and share his employer's ultimate dream for the Multnomah: that it would be the most prestigious and sought-after accommodation and gathering place in Portland, with a reputation for giving its customers only the best of service.

Stinson, with Hauser's blessing and apparent input, set out to accomplish his goal by first striving to develop an esprit de corps that would imbue the staff with a desire and the means to become a very real part of a worthwhile endeavor; i.e., to offer the best service possible to the customer. To achieve this goal, Stinson hired individuals who would care about their jobs and be proud of the work they would do at and for the Multnomah. Evidently, he succeeded: soon men and women were hired who would spend the next 20, 30, and even 40 or more years at the Multnomah. Some of the staff became institutions in their own right. Rose Petzoldt, who began June 23, 1917, as a maid in the housekeeping department, worked seven days a week at $25 per month and took care of 30 rooms! Rose eventually moved up to the sewing room, then the linen room, and in 1936 was made head housekeeper. She retained this position until 1942, when she partially retired, but continued on as a part-time banquet waitress until retiring in 1961, thus ending a 44-year career at the Multnomah.

Hipolito Dacang was hired in August of 1919 as a bus boy, then a dining room waiter and then a room-service waiter in 1946. He worked at the Multnomah for a grand total of 42 years!

Hans Rampmeier, who began in 1921, worked for over 40 years as the head bellman. Genuinely liked and admired by both the staff and the guests, Rampmeier was the Multnomah's unofficial photographer; many of the extant photos of Multnomah employees are from his collection. In an interview in the employee newsletter, on the occasion of his 40th anniversary, Rampmeier remembered vividly many of the important and interesting guests the Multnomah had hosted during his tenure: Mary Pickford, Rudolph Valentino, Lana Turner, Henry Cabot Lodge, Marshalls Foch and Petain of France, and Generals John J. Pershing and George Marshall of the United States.

Historical Photograph Collecions, Washington State University Libraries

Photo of Joan Crawford autographed for Hans Rampmeier at the Multnomah Hotel, Portland, Oregon.

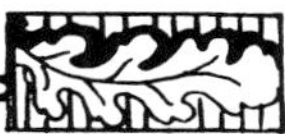

Hal Carey Collection

The Story of the Stars and the bellmen staff

Some of the staff's relatives were so impressed by the steady work the Multnomah provided and the camaraderie among the employees that they, too, joined the hotel's ranks. Anna Petzoldt joined her sister, Rose, in the linen room, and worked at the Multnomah almost as long as Rose. They and other Multnomah employees lived by the advice of F. G. Odell, which Hauser had published in an early employee newsletter, the "Multnomah Review," in 1918. According to Odell, the "key to the modern hotel business is service; considering the guests' interest first . . . good service requires imagination, interest and attention–to put yourself in the guest's place first."

Hauser, Stinson, and subsequent managers of the Multnomah worked hard to reward the employees who followed this advice. They began the Multnomah's tradition of employee newsletters, which kept the staff informed about the hotel's day-to-day business. They rewarded work well done by promotions and public notice. Employees who worked five and ten years were presented with Multnomah commemorative pins. Holidays were important at the Multnomah, not only for the guests, but

for the staff, who were invited and encouraged to participate in festive dinners and parties. For as long as Hauser owned the hotel, this tradition of valuing the employees' role in the hotel's success continued and was largely responsible for that success.

Marketing and Promotions Efforts

Hauser was also astute enough to continue the marketing, publicity, and promotions efforts begun by Bowers and Goldstein under Gevurtz and Yates. He was well aware that his own connections with Sam Hill, James J. Hill, and Portland's leaders were instrumental in attracting many of Portland's well-known visitors as guests of the Multnomah. During Hauser's ownership, the most famous of these were the visit in 1926 of Queen Marie of Romania and of Charles A. Lindbergh in 1927. When Sam Hill learned that Marshall Joffre, whom he had met in France during World War I, would be lecturing in America, he invited him to Portland and arranged for him to stay at the Multnomah. Hill also invited Chief Poker Jim from Pendleton, the chief of the Oregon Native Americans who had volunteered in the U.S. Army and fought in France. Hauser was happy to host welcoming banquets and activities for these famous guests, and always managed to get at least a photograph of himself with the notable visitors into the newspapers.

Hauser also continued the Gevurtz tradition of the early owners and managers who became members of Portland's most prestigious clubs and societies. Along with joining the Arlington Club, Portland's exclusive

Oregon Historical Society Negative Number OrHi 24217-A

Eric V. Hauser receiving Indian delegation in 1922

men's club, Hauser also invited the newly formed Rose Festival Association to make the Multnomah its headquarters. Thus, from 1920, when Hauser was elected president of the Rose Festival Association, to the late 1950s, the Rose Festival not only had its offices in the Multnomah but also held all the Rose Festival ceremonies, including the crowning of the King and Queen of Rosaria, at the hotel. Hauser generously donated the throne he had commissioned for Queen Marie to the Rose Festival for the queen's crowning ceremony; it was used for many years by the Rose Festival Association. When other clubs began reserving the Multnomah for their official meetings and annual functions, these activities not only ensured peak occupancy during the week but acted as a magnet drawing the local citizenry to inspect the hotel's charms and explore its potential as a suitable setting for family dinners and entertainment and for celebrating weddings, anniversaries, and other happy occasions.

Service Standards High

Hauser was careful to give conventioneers full access to all the services offered by the hotel. He

Wedding at the Multnomah Hotel ballroom
Photo from Oregon Historical Society's
Chinn family collection

Oregon Historical Society Negative Number CN 015410

Multnomah Hotel Orchestra

Oregon Historical Society Negative Number OrHi 82926

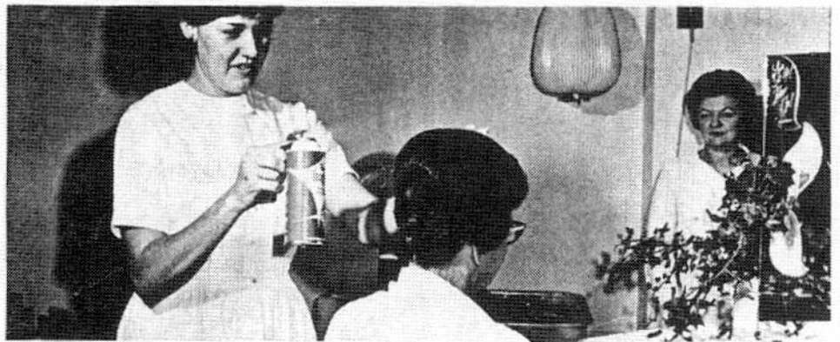

1. Ilene's Salon of Beauty

A new five-minute hair drier now makes it possible for Milady to have a shampoo, setting and styling all in 45 minutes, reports Owner Ilene Copeland.

The *six operators* in the shop are all top hair stylists, and offer complete hair services and manicures. Miss Copeland, herself, was trained in England and Canada, and is well up on the latest European and American hair stylings.

Ilene's Salon of Beauty is open from 8 to 5:30 six days a week. Evening appointments are also available.

2. The Barber Shop

Co-owners H.D. Bienert and Duke Owens are justifiably proud of their establishment, which offers complete services for the well-groomed man - haircuts, shaves, facial, massage, shampoo. The shop specializes in razor cutting and a new "shape wave" shampoo, during which the customer never leaves his chair.

The waiting and cutting rooms are separate. The city's best shoe shine is available at the shop, and the five-barber staff means there is little, if any, waiting. Appointments are accepted and encouraged, which puts you in the barber chair the minute you walk through the door.

3.The Multnomah Pharmacy

Owner Jack Davis set up shop in The Multnomah in June of 1927, and has been here ever since.

The pharmacy offers a full prescription service, plus drugs and toiletries, news stand, tobacco products and greeting cards.

The well-stocked gift department specializes in myrtlewood items, delightful presents to bring home to the wife and family.

Jack Davis has made many, many friends during his 37 Multnomah years and, as he says over and over, "I've enjoyed every minute of it." And so has The Multnomah.

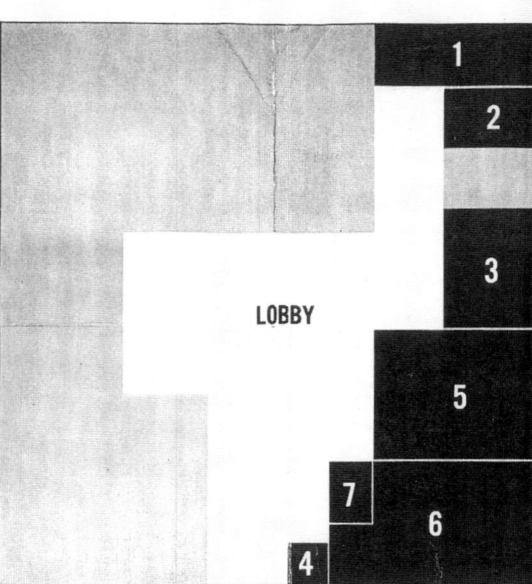

4. Imperial Travel Bureau

World-wide travel and reservation services are quickly and efficiently arranged for through the Imperial Travel Bureau in The Multnomah. Included in this broad category are convention sightseeing tours, river trips, Grayline area tours and Avis car rentals.

Miss Kathy Baker, manager, points out that the travel bureau will obtain tickets for steamship and rail travel anywhere in the world, and will write tickets direct for air and bus travel.

Travelers checks can be purchased through the bureau as well. And, finally, if you have a few extra minutes, come in and browse among the hundreds of travel and hotel folders on display - you can dream, can't you?

5. Ray Bolger's Men's Shop

Sartorial elegance is the by-word at The Multnomah's new men's shop, owned and operated by Portland's own Ray Bolger, who has been in the business for 27 years.

Managed by Frank German, the tastefully decorated store offers a complete line of men's suits and sportswear, shoes, furnishings and gifts.

Custom tailoring - for which Bolger is nationally known - is also available at The Multnomah clothing store. Whether it's a complete suit of clothes or a set of cuff links, you'll find the best of the line at Ray Bolger's.

6. The Leather Shop

This fine leather store has been a part of The Multnomah since 1938, turning out hand-made leather goods equal to none.

Owner Rudy Casperson is a craftsman with a wide reputation, and his customers keep returning from all over the world. Specializing in deerskin goods, the shop features handmade slippers, belts, purses, billfolds and jackets, plus a broad line of other leather goods such as boots and moccasins.

If your luggage needs repairing, bring it in for a quick -and excellent- leather repair job. And don't fail to ask about the "Chuck-A-Boot," a Multnomah Leather Shop special.

7.Tommy Luke's Flower Shop

Complete floral arrangements for conventions, dignitaries, center pieces, banquets and show rooms are provided by this elegant flower shop in The Multnomah.

And that's only a part of the service, according to Manager Nolan Lawer. You can send flowers anywhere in the world from The Multnomah, or order a corsage made while you wait. Three feet or three thousand miles - your order will be fresh and fragrant every time.

Tommy Luke's also puts on floral demonstrations for convention wives or ladies' groups meeting in the hotel.

Courtesy of Mark Casperson

Brochure showing location and description of shops in the Multnomah Hotel (1964)

saw to it that the dining and banquet room menus were lavish and he emphasized the small touches that endeared the Multnomah to its guests. Each evening, for example, the currency taken in that day was laundered and ironed and the coins were polished! Doormen not only opened the doors for the guests and relieved them of their wet coats and umbrellas but saw to it they were dry by the time the guests departed. Room service was available at any hour, and room service waiters knew how to be discreet when situations called for discretion. Wallace Beery, the famous comedian, who stayed at the Multnomah for a long period of time, had the habit of sitting in the lobby in his shirtsleeves for several hours, even taking an occasional nap. When it was no longer appropriate for him to occupy space in the lobby, Hans Rampmeier always called a page boy to escort Beery to his room to finish his daily siesta.

The Multnomah also encouraged Portland businesses to establish their offices in the hotel's lobby and on the mezzanine, especially those that could provide guests with services the Multnomah did not. Both women and men could have their coiffures taken care of by the hotel's beauty and barber shops; a boot black, tobacco shop, and newsstand were permanently located in the lobby. Beginning in the early '20s, the hotel always had a florist shop, and Portland businessman, Tommy Luke finally found a profitable enterprise in the florist shop he located in the Multnomah.

The hotel also offered accommodations for businesses needing street-level access. From the building's opening in 1912, Matson Steamship Lines had their offices in the Multnomah Building. Alex and Baldwin Steamship Accountants also leased space in the Multnomah and were instrumental in bringing in the Hawaii Steamship Lines and the Oceanic and Orient Navigation Company.

Other companies and services operated elsewhere in the hotel, including the Turkish baths in the basement, the Multnomah Hotel Travel Company, Hauser Construction Company, and a public stenographer on the mezzanine. The Rose Festival Association had its own suite of rooms on the second floor, as did various lawyers and engineers operating one-man firms.

Under Hauser's leadership, the Multnomah was a bustling, busy place, and by the time he died in 1929, the Multnomah had established its place as the leading hotel in Portland, the "Grand Old Lady of Fourth Avenue." Hauser was able to realize his dream of prominence and respectability by the standards he set, the service he provided, and the spirit he engendered within the Multnomah Hotel. In turn, the Multnomah's guests from all over the United States, indeed, the world, spread the word far and wide that this relatively modest hotel, located in an area of the United States that was not widely known, ranked with the best for its hospitality, friendliness, and welcome to strangers.

Hauser's Death

Eric V. Hauser, Sr., died in February, 1929, after a short, unexpected illness. He had become ill after the Thanksgiving holidays and was hospitalized for several days in St. Vincent Hospital, a short distance west of the Multnomah Hotel. At his bedside when he died were his son, Eric, Jr., and his long-time friend, R.R. Budd, president of the Great Northern Railroad. His wife, who had made the last of her annual visits the previous summer, was at their home in St. Paul when her husband died. She did come to Portland for the funeral.

In his will, Hauser bequeathed several substantial sums to local colleges. He left Albany College (later moved to Portland and renamed Lewis and Clark College) $100,000, and gave smaller grants to Reed College and Monmouth College. Several of his brothers received bequests, and the St. Paul estate was willed to his wife. Hauser Construction was left to his children, as was the Multnomah Hotel and other hotel interests he held in Oregon.

The middle son, Kenneth, had been working for the U.S. Corps of Engineers in Washington, D.C. A gifted engineer, Kenneth took over the management of Hauser Construction Company, eventually buying out his siblings and gaining sole ownership. Kenneth continued Hauser Construction's railroad work, built jetties on the southern Oregon coast, and did engineering work for the government during World War II.

Norma Hauser's husband, Bill Faricy, took over Hauser Securities, the entity which owned the Multnomah Hotel. He and Rupert Hauser bought property in Los Angeles and Canada to grow food and wheat to sell overseas, primarily to Armenia. The company they began with their Canadian partners still operates out of Calgary, Alberta.

After his father's death, Eric Jr., took responsibility for the Multnomah. His management style was similar to his father's and he very much wished to keep the Multnomah's reputation and style. He also owned an interest in Portland's Heathman Hotel and other hotels throughout Oregon.

The Hauser children remained in Portland, but their mother returned to St. Paul. Eric Hauser, Sr. had achieved his dream. He died well-to-do and, more importantly, respected. His legacy, the Multnomah Hotel, remains as a lasting monument to his life and goals.

Sam Hill
Friend and Promoter of the Multnomah

No account of Eric Hauser's success at the Multnomah would be complete without a further glimpse into the role played by Sam Hill in that success. Samuel Hill was born in North Carolina in 1857, the son of Quaker parents. In 1865, the family moved to St. Paul, Minnesota, where Sam lived until he entered Haverford College just outside Philadelphia, Pennsylvania. After graduation, he attended Harvard

Oregon Historical Society Negative Number CN-18315

Samuel Hill with his "trademark" globe

Law School and received his law degree in 1886. His first job was in the legal department of the Great Northern Railroad. Two years later, in 1888, he married Mary Frances Hill, the eldest daughter of James J. Hill, chairman of the Great Northern Railway Company. Their first child, Mary Mendenhall Hill, was born in 1889 and was later joined by a brother.

Intelligent and eccentric, handsome with a full head of hair and a thick mustache, Samuel Hill first became aware of the beauty of the Pacific Northwest after his father-in-law, James Hill, appointed him a director of the Great Northern Railway. Early on, Sam played a key role in the construction of the Spokane, Portland & Seattle Line (SP&S), a subsidiary of the Great Northern, and on his first trip to the Northwest to help lay out the line, he was overwhelmed by the beauty of the region. Against his wife's wishes, he persuaded James Hill to transfer him permanently to the Northwest to oversee the operation of the SP&S.

Sam appeared to be poised to succeed his father-in-law as chairman of the GN when much to everyone's surprise, he quit GN in 1900 and moved to Seattle. There he headed the Seattle Gas & Electric Company and began to indulge his passion for travel and adventure. He became a food distributor, brokering sales of northwest wheat and other agricultural products to European and South American markets. Because of his previous connection with the SP&S and GN railways, he was able to arrange rail shipments of his products via the SP&S/GN network at competitive prices.

Raised as a Quaker, Hill was greatly disturbed by the Great War in which all of Europe and the United States was engulfed from 1914–1917. Philosophically opposed to the idea of war, he was also deeply moved by the suffering of the innocent people caught up in the slaughter, as well as by the deaths of hundreds of thousands of soldiers. His travels in Europe, while lucrative for his business, opened his eyes to the devastating results of the war to end all wars. He became convinced that he had a duty to advance the cause of nonviolence and that if all peoples would only come together in harmony and peace, then never again would the world have to endure another catastrophe like World War I.

His conviction soon took shape in a "House of Peace." In 1907, Hill had purchased 7,000 acres in Washington State in an area known as Columbus, high on a cliff overlooking the Columbia River. With unobstructed views of the magnificent gorge, Mt. Hood, Mt. St. Helens, and Mt. Adams, this spot was ideal, Hill thought, for a Quaker community and a monument to peace and artistic beauty.

Even before the war ended, Hill began construction of "Maryhill," named for his wife and daughter, on his cliff, at whose base ran the SP&S railroad line. Hill's plan was to construct a museum, large enough to hold contributions from his friends all over the world and artworks and manuscripts donated by governments pledged to promote harmony between all nations.

Before construction was completed, donations from the sculptor Rodin, a statue of Diana given by the people of France to the people of the United States, and other artworks from Belgium, Greece, Russia, and Romania began to fill up the museum.

Despite Sam's world-wide travels and his friendship with individuals far removed from the type of life most Oregonians and Washingtonians lived (even the wealthy ones), he was never happier than when he came home to the Northwest. After starting construction on Maryhill, he regarded that as his home, but as it remained unfinished during his lifetime, he usually lived in his home in Seattle or came down to Portland to stay with his friend and sometime partner, Eric Hauser. Gregarious and an extrovert, as opposed to Hauser's rather stern and remote manner, Sam enjoyed his sojourns at the Multnomah where his friend and others were always ready to discuss an idea or a business deal. The two friends often found that their mutual interests resulted in profitable money-making deals.

Over the years, Hill and Hauser forged a strong friendship based on their business interests, their love of the Northwest, and their desire to win prominence and respectability. Sam found in Hauser someone with whom he could share his dreams. Although the naturally reticent Hauser seldom reciprocated, Sam was never embarrassed or afraid to pour out his heart to his friend, sharing with him his frustrations in failing to get the Oregon legislature to appropriate funds for a highway through the Willamette Valley and his hurt and disappointment that his family refused to join him in the Northwest. In this instance, Hauser could commiserate with understanding since his own wife seldom visited Portland.

Courtesy of the Maryhill Museum

Sam Hill's Maryhill with the Columbia River Gorge in the background

Sam was well liked by the staff of the Multnomah, and when he was expected there was a great rush to prepare the Governor's suite with fresh flowers and crisp linens. He was always ready with a quick laugh at a joke, an admiring gaze at a photograph of a new baby, and a congratulations for a job well done to a five-year employee. He tipped generously, and generally endeared himself to everyone from the chef, whom he always summoned to compliment on a fine dinner, to the first violinist who played a particularly lovely solo in the Arcadian Garden, to the maid who always made sure his bed was turned down, and to the shoeshine boy who insisted on giving his hat and boots a quick brush each day.

Eric Hauser first heard about Sam's friend, Queen Marie of Romania, a year or two before she came to America. In one late-night outpouring, Sam spent hours telling his friend of her beauty, her regard for her subjects, her eye for fine art, her ear for music, and her despair at the devastation the war had caused in her country. Sam was convinced the queen was his soul-mate and he desperately hoped that she would come to love him as he loved her. It was common knowledge, he told Hauser, that the queen's marriage was in name only, and he felt that he could have a chance to win her love. Sympathetic to his friend's yearning, Hauser advised Sam to keep in contact with Queen Marie but warned that he would be asking a lot of the queen to give up her marriage and her title, no matter how unhappy she was. Whenever Sam returned to the Multnomah, Hauser always asked him about his relations with the queen, but, alas, there was never any change. Then, one day, Sam triumphantly telegraphed Hauser that Marie was coming to America to dedicate his Maryhill! He promised he would introduce her to Hauser and would try to get her to come to Portland and stay at the Multnomah!

Oregon Historical Society Negative Number OrHi 72864

The banner to the left of the building advertises the Elks Club International Convention, July 1912; the Multnomah's first convention.

Courtesy of Maryhill Museum

The lovely Marie of Romania, a strong monarch, loyal friend, and beautiful woman who captured Sam Hill's heart. She was the first royal personage to visit Portland (1926) where she stayed at the Multnomah Hotel.

QUEEN MARIE OF ROMANIA and SAM HILL

Sam Hill Meets Queen Marie

Hill first met the popular Queen Marie of Romania on one of his trips to Europe in the early 1920s, when he was delivering food for the Red Cross to war refugees in the Balkans. Marie was an ardent sponsor of the Red Cross, and whenever she could, she took the opportunity to volunteer her services to the wounded Romanian soldiers and her devastated subjects attempting to rebuild their lives. Despite Marie's position as queen and her marriage to Ferdinand, Hill fell madly in love with her and even hoped one day to marry her. He grasped every opportunity to be with her, following her to Romania, France, and wherever he could meet her. Though his wealth made him attractive to many, some of the roy-

alty snubbed him as a crass American "trying to buy European culture." But Queen Marie genuinely enjoyed his company especially their philosophical discussions about the importance of peace and the restoration of Europe. As they grew closer, Sam kept hoping that he could persuade her to come to America to see the Pacific Northwest, and Maryhill, his House of Peace.

The hoped-for opportunity came in 1926, when the Romanian government arranged for Queen Marie to make a state visit to key cities in the United States. Arriving in New York, the queen began a carefully planned tour, dining at Mount Vernon with the first lady, Mrs. Coolidge, speaking in Philadelphia, and then, crossing the country in a private train to California, Spokane, and Seattle. Sam had persuaded the queen to detour to Maryhill, where she would stop long enough to dedicate the House of Peace and to celebrate its opening with Sam and the many dignitaries from Washington and Oregon. The enterprising Sam also arranged an unscheduled side-trip to Portland to honor his friend, Eric Hauser, proprietor of the Multnomah Hotel, and to meet other local civic leaders, his society friends, and railroad associates. The queen not only agreed to Sam's plan but also gave him carte blanche to arrange the details for the western stage of the trip. Most importantly to Sam, she permitted him to be at her side during this trip to the Pacific Northwest.

A Popular Monarch

Who was this woman who so captivated the wealthy Sam Hill that he ignored the whispers of his peers as he trailed the royal entourage? Queen Marie of Romania, English-born daughter of Alfred, Duke of Edinburgh and Grand Duchess Marie Alexandrovna of Russia, and great-granddaughter of Queen Victoria, was a strong and serious monarch who, with her husband, Ferdinand I, successfully guided the small kingdom of Romania through the perils of the First World War. Ascending the throne with Ferdinand in 1914, Marie took advantage of her relationship with her first cousins, George V of England and Nicholas II of Russia, to persuade her husband to join the Allied cause and then acted as trusted envoy between them and another first cousin, Kaiser Wilhelm, of Germany.

After the war, in addition to her official duties and Red Cross work, Marie became a roving ambassador for her adopted country, traveling throughout Europe as part of the contingent of international and wealthy jet setters. Marie's popularity won her dozens of invitations from her European friends. At balls, banquets, and cultural affairs, she was widely admired. In the words of one reporter, "she came and she conquered by the heavy force of her personality." Mother to Crown Prince Carol, Princess Elisabetha, Princess Marie (Mignon), Prince Nicholas, and Princess Ileana, five of the most eligible royal offspring (another boy, Mircea, had died in 1916 at the age of three), Marie also felt obliged to forge international alliances and friendships in order to give her children and her country every advantage in the international marriage game.

A Promising Beginning

The royal visit to the Northwest was scheduled for November 3–4, 1926. Dazzled by this opportunity to escort his royal friend, Sam spared no cost and quickly named a committee of influential Portlanders to schedule a tour that would highlight the city's most attractive features. A group of 25 Romanian ex-patriots, led by Adolph Feldstein, would be the first to greet the queen at the Multnomah Hotel. E. A. Stuart, president of the Portland International Livestock Exposition, and Eric V. Hauser, a board member, arranged a special evening at the annual Portland Horse Show in honor of the queen.

Hill himself took care of the arrangements at Maryhill. Despite the fact that the museum was not finished (indeed, it was an empty shell of concrete and steel and unplastered walls!), he uncrated dozens of pieces of artwork and brought in furnishings and decorations to make the building more attractive. He chose the Romanian Room in which to hold the dedication, the first of what he hoped would be many such dedications to peace. Hill chose evergreens and chrysanthemums to decorate the Romanian Room and delegated ten society matrons to be his hostesses. They and a press corps were to motor up to Maryhill the

Courtesy of Maryhill Museum

Her majesty, Queen Marie of Romania

night before. Sam personally selected the luncheon menu and chose Portland's Mayor Baker to give the welcoming speech. First, Sam would introduce the queen at the dedication; then she would address the assembled dignitaries and citizens of Klickitat County from the balcony of the Romanian Room.

The Multnomah Prepares

Meanwhile, the Multnomah was busy getting ready for the most illustrious visitor it had ever received. Eric Hauser volunteered his establishment as headquarters for the queen and her entourage. Always ready to be at the forefront of Portland's social elite, Hauser spared no expense to ready the hotel for Portland's first royal guests which included the queen's children, Princess Ileana and Prince Nicholas. Thirty rooms on the second floor were painted and decorated for the royal party. Special attention was given to the corner suite (No. 23) which the queen would occupy.

At his friend Sam's urging, Hauser commissioned a 10-piece matching set of fruitwood furniture for the queen's private suite. Handmade in France, the set was valued at $10,000 and consisted of twin beds, night stands, chests of drawers, a dining set, writing and side tables and chairs. A throne was built so that the queen would be comfortable in familiar surroundings. The queen's private bathroom was even equipped with a new commode, one shaped, no less, like a throne! Other rooms were royally decorated to accommodate the prince and princess.

Before dawn on Wednesday, November 3, 1926, the Multnomah was in high gear. In all its fourteen years, it had never played host to royalty. Presidents, yes: Teddy Roosevelt had spoken at the Multnomah in 1912, and FDR had stayed while on a vice-presidential campaign tour in 1919. Generals, sometimes: French generals Foch, Joffre, and Petain has been guests after World War I, as had American generals Marshall and Pershing. As impressive as these guests were, they did not excite Portlanders as much as the prospect of entertaining royalty!

Manager Richard W. Childs, who had first come to the Multnomah in 1921 as publicity manager, had his troops working hard by 5:30 a.m. the morning of the queen's arrival A whirlwind of activity had preceded the royal visit by several weeks, and Childs now looked forward to a very exhausting day.

The French furniture had been delivered directly from the docks only two days before. The beds, tables, chests of drawers, and dining suite needed a final dusting; Childs wondered who in the housekeeping staff could take care of it.

The head housekeeper was busy arranging the flowers for the royal suite. Local Portland florists had begun delivering flowers the previous Monday. Big standards of roses and rhododendrons had already been placed around the lobby. Portland, the City of Roses, would outdo itself in supplying Queen Marie with the beauty and fragrance of the city's finest symbol.

In the kitchen, the head chef and pastry chef were disappointed to learn that there would be no grand banquet to prepare. But there would be a formal dinner and luncheon and plenty to do to make sure that anything the royal party would care to eat or drink would be available.

Hans Rampmeier, head bellman, had the day-shift bell staff polishing furniture, brass fittings, and glass chandeliers in between escorting guests and carrying bags. Two page boys were sweeping the sidewalk in front of the main entrance on Pine Street in preparation for laying the new red carpet. Their job throughout the day was to make sure the carpet remained clean!

Hans also had to deal with the logistics of transferring the mountains of royal luggage from the train to the hotel. His experience with important guests had taught him that the more famous the guest, the more luggage he or she had. Since he had seen the photos of the queen's wardrobe published earlier in *The Oregonian*, he knew that she and Princess Ileana would have many pieces of luggage. Add to these Prince Nicholas' bags and those of the royal attendants, and Hans knew he would have his hands full.

Rampmeier decided to dispatch three or four private cars along with the hotel's car to the depot, which was less than a mile each way. If each car made two or three trips, it would take about two to three hours to transfer the bags.

Courtesy Washington State University Libraries

Her Majesty's boudoir

Her Majesty's parlor

Courtesy Washington State University Libraries

Courtesy Washington State University Libraries

Her Majesty's drawing room

Rampmeier could only hope that the baggage would arrive in Portland well before the queen and her party were scheduled to arrive by car from the Columbia River Gorge.

Hipolito Dacang, a seven-year veteran of the dining-room staff, was assigned the task of readying the china, flatware, and crystal which would be carried up to the royal suite. Polishing silver and wiping glasses, Hipolito was hoping to catch a glimpse of the royal party's arrival later that afternoon.

Down in the laundry room, Rose Petzold was pressing out the last wrinkles in the new sheets that were to go on the royal beds. Rose had laundered these sheets the day before to make them soft and comfortable for the queen and her children. While she ironed, Rose wondered what the queen would be like. Rumors had been flying around the hotel that Sam Hill, a favorite with all the staff, was in love with the queen and had persuaded her to come to Portland to show her his world and ask her to be part of it. Since Sam's wife, Mary, and his children chose to remain in St. Paul and Chicago rather than to live at Maryhill or Portland, it was a well-known secret that the popular Sam Hill wanted someone with whom to share his dreams and ideals.

The Royal Visit

The royal visit began with the queen's train arriving at Maryhill during the early morning hours of Wednesday, November 3. Arising after daylight, the party attended a breakfast at 9:30 at the Meadowlark Inn, an occasion that was less organized than Sam would have wished. According to Gladys Bowman, a reporter for *The Oregonian,* the inn was not equipped to handle the overwhelming numbers in the entourage. To everyone's amazement, the queen and her children ended up in the kitchen where Marie cooked and served pancakes to Sam and her children! Breakfast over, the party motored the two miles to Maryhill where, standing outside on the bal-

Courtesy of Maryhill Museum

Courtesy of Maryhill Museum

Crowds stood waiting for hours at the dedication ceremony.

Courtesy of Maryhill Museum

The fields surrounding the Maryhill were covered with the automobiles of the news reporters, well-wishers and the curious.

Courtesy of Maryhill Museum

Releasing the doves at the dedication of Maryhill by Queen Marie of Romania

cony despite the cold and bitter wind, and looking down on over five thousand spectators, Marie formally dedicated the edifice to world peace: a world of "dreams, work, love and friendship." She concluded: "There is a dream built into this place—a dream for today and for tomorrow as well."

Sam spoke of the queen and "her womanly qualities which always win the praise of peoples no matter in what station they may be," and told of the noble purpose for which she was crossing an ocean and a continent. That purpose, he stated, was to "perform a queenly part in making possible a treasure for art and works, a treasure of international good will." Privately, Sam also hoped that one day Marie would consent to live with him at Maryhill.

After the dedication, the party entrained for the trip to Portland. Crossing into Oregon at Celilo Falls, the train stopped on the SP&S bridge for lunch. The queen and her children, the newspaper reported, were delighted with the novelty of the locale and the breathtaking beauty of the river. After lunch, the party transferred to open cars on the Oregon side, and began the ride down the Columbia River Highway, stopping for ten minutes for a quick reception in The Dalles. The cavalcade officially entered Portland at N.E. Sandy Boulevard at 82nd Street. Because Portland's mayor and Oregon's governor had attended the ceremonies at Maryhill and were in the caravan, no ceremonies were held when the queen entered Portland.

Portland's Chamber of Commerce saw to it that the route into the city was decorated with flowers and marked with throngs of cheering people. All government buildings flew the flag of Romania while the 30-car entourage made a hurried tour of the east- and

west-side business districts. Originally, the queen was to have been driven up Terwilliger Boulevard to the Hillvilla Restaurant which had a spectacular view of the Willamette River and the city's east side. But as they neared the Multnomah Hotel, Marie whispered to Sam that she was tired and wished to stop for a rest. The royal wish being Sam's command, the city tour was cut short and they hurried to the hotel. Here the Romanian ex-patriots held a welcoming ceremony before a throng of people eager to catch sight of the royalty. The queen, her children, and Sam dined with Eric Hauser, Mayor Baker, and other friends before they were scheduled to attend the Portland Horse Show at 9:30 that evening.

Sam is Disappointed

Later that night, as the party left the Multnomah Hotel to attend the Portland Horse Show, Sam and two of Marie's official aides had an altercation. Major Stanley Washburn and Colonel John H. Carroll argued with Sam over who was to ride with the queen. Sam had arranged that he and Oregon's Governor Pierce would accompany the queen to the horse show, but before either could enter her car, Major Washburn shoved them aside and slammed the door, forcing the governor and Sam to take the next car. Sam regarded this as a gross insult, not only to the governor but to himself, and as the party entered the royal box, he argued heatedly with Washburn and Carroll. The two men left

Courtesy of Maryhill Museum

Dinner given by Eric V. Hauser for Her Majesty Marie, Queen of Romania at the Multnomah Hotel, November 3, 1926. Seated to the right of Queen Marie are Sam Hill, and to his right, Princess Ileana. To the Queen's left are Portland's Mayor Baker, Mrs. Baker, and Prince Nicholas.

the box, but not before a photographer had snapped a picture of the argument. An account was published in *The Oregonian* the next day.

Despite the unpleasantness, Queen Marie and her children enjoyed the horse show, catching the Multnomah Hotel's $2,000 Stakes race for three-gaited saddle horses, but the altercation and the lateness of the hour prompted the queen to return prematurely to the hotel. Later that night, Marie met with Sam. He spoke to her of his dream that she would embrace his world, publicly acknowledge their friendship, and give him some indication that she cared more than casually for him. Alas, she gently explained to him that she could not give up her duty to her husband and her people. Furthermore, she did not embrace the rustic quality of the northwest as he did, and, unfortunately, she simply did not feel for him anything other than friendship. Crushed and hurt, Sam never recovered from his unrequited love.

No official account was ever released of their discussion, but Sam took his leave of the queen and the hotel. The next day the royal party continued on to Seattle with Colonel Carroll and Major Washburn resuming control of the queen's agenda.

Carroll later announced on behalf of the queen that "Her Majesty had thoroughly enjoyed the reception in the far West and hoped to be able to make another visit later." She never did.

A Lasting Monument

Begun in 1917, Maryhill was not completed until 1940, after Sam's death. He willed $1.2 million to maintain his "House of Peace," which remains today as a remarkable acknowledgment of one man's hope for unity and peace among nations, as well as a repository of local artifacts and treasures. In 1930, Sam had also built a replica of Stonehenge several miles to the east of Maryhill in honor of the Klickitat veterans of World War I. It, too, remains a popular monument attracting thousands of visitors annually. The Quaker community Sam had envisioned was never built.

Marie died in 1938 without realizing her promise to return sometime to the United States. Nicholas, exiled by his elder brother, King Carol, in 1937, lived the remainder of his life in Switzerland. Princess Ileana, after her first husband, a royal prince, died, left Romania in 1948 with her six children. Eventually reaching the United States, she founded a monastery in Pennsylvania and became its mother general, Mother Alexandra. Her long, eventful life ended with her death in 1996.

The story of the relationship between Sam Hill and Queen Marie, part fact, part fiction, is still interwoven with the history of the Multnomah Hotel as told by those who were there. Sam's romance with Marie, while never officially acknowledged in any biography or history written about either of them, was a fact that was obvious to the hotel staff but may have been embellished by Eric Hauser. The story that Sam had been spurned by Marie is speculation by the author but one that can claim to be a logical conclusion based on the accounts of the time in the newspapers and the reminiscences of the hotel employees.

© Curt Teich Postcard Archives Lake County (IL) Museum

Early colorized postcard advertising the Multnomah Hotel

Oregon Historical Society Negative Number OrHi 82928

Early conventioneers at the Multnomah Hotel in 1925

Oregon Historical Society Negative Number OrHi 96215
A home merchandising conference in the dining room of the Multnomah Hotel–1938

Oregon Historical Society Negative Number OrHi 8166-A
The International Teamsters' Convention at the Multnomah Hotel–September 10, 1935

Oregon Historical Society Negative Number OrHi 96212
Touring the new kitchen facilities and sampling the food prepared by head pantryman Dick Douglas

WESTERN INTERNATIONAL HOTELS A LONG AND PROFITABLE ASSOCIATION

Gordon Bass, who was a major resource for the author's account of the Multnomah Hotel, briefly outlined the following history of Western International Hotels. One of Western's oldest employees, Mr. Bass died in June, 1996, at the age of 86, and with his passing a good part of the company's history has been lost. Some of what remains of Mr. Bass' and Western's story follows.

In 1910, two Spokane, Washington, businessmen, S.W. Thurston and H.S. Maltby, formed a partnership. From 1910 to 1930, the Maltby-Thurston Company established a reputation for turning unprofitable hotels in the Spokane-Seattle area into profitable enterprises. Together, the two men capitalized on Maltby's hotel experience and Thurston's managerial knowledge and cash outlay.

Buying, selling, and leasing many hotels, they continued to increase their stature and revenues. Their modus operandi was based on the principle of the three **Is**:

Integrity–which enabled them to secure credit;

Intestinal Fortitude–which encouraged them to seek out new properties, new ideas and concepts, and to carry them through;

Intelligence–a helpful guide in choosing partners who were reliable, honest, and enterprising.

The three **Is** by which the founders operated, remained, in Mr. Bass's words, "very, very much in the company throughout its history."

Washington Hoteliers Form Management Company

In 1930, it seemed prudent for Maltby and Thurston to look for new partners to strengthen and deepen the company's resources as a defense against the worsening economy. Guided by the three **Is**, they brought in four more men of intelligence, integrity and intestinal fortitude: the brothers Frank and Hal Dupar and Peter and Adolph Schmidt. The Dupars, plumbing and construction contractors in Spokane, had begun their careers in San Francisco around the time of the 1906 earthquake. After moving to Washington, the Dupars built the Hungerford Hotel in Seattle and the Cascadian in Wenatchee. Soon after completing the Cascadian, they were forced to manage it in order to defray their construction costs.

The Schmidt brothers came from the family which owned the Olympia Brewery in Olympia, the state's capitol city. They had gone into the hotel business because prohibition had forced them to search out private outlets for their beer. Five hotels were operated by the brothers: the Governor and Olympian Hotels in Olympia, the Henry and Leopold Hotels in Bellingham, and the New Washington in Seattle.

The six rival entrepreneurs–the two Dupars, the two Schmidts, and Thurston and Maltby–had never considered a merger of their common interests. Then one day, Thurston and Frank Dupar met by chance at a coffee shop in Yakima. Both were trying to negotiate a deal on the steel framework of an abandoned building that had served for 20 years no better purpose than as a pigeon roost. After their meeting, Thurston and Dupar decided to bury the hatchet. They formulated a plan to work together rather than to fight against each other and later contacted the Schmidts, who also agreed to work with their former rivals.

The six men, representing three of the most active and powerful hotel companies in Washington, moved forward quickly on their merger so that they could improve their businesses. Their primary goals were to stabilize rates, combine and standardize accounting procedures (Hal Dupar formulated the first food-cost system), combine purchasing, and direct business to one another.

Because they could not agree on the respective values of each of their properties, the six partners decided to establish a joint management contract that would allow them to retain separate ownership of their existing properties. Naming their new entity the Western Hotel Company, the owners agreed that their management group would control management policies and would charge a fee for its services. In addition, the firm would own no stock or interest in any single property and at the end of each fiscal year would split any profits among those "who had done the work and carried the load," an important concept that remains a hallmark of the company even today.

Western Hotel Company

Thus, the Western Hotel Company, formed in 1930, became the manager of fifteen of the most prominent hotels in the Northwest. The company's flagship hotels were the New Washington in Seattle and the Benjamin Franklin in Spokane. Of the founding members, Thurston became president and Frank Dupar, secretary; the other four held various offices. A young man, Eddie Carlson, was hired as page boy at the Benjamin Franklin, his first job.

Only one year later, 1931, Western made the first of many significant moves that contributed to its world-wide success. That year, Eric Hauser, Jr., was looking for a company to manage the hotel he and his brothers and sister had inherited from their

PORTLAND'S LARGEST AND NATIONALLY FAMOUS HOSTELRY

● Offers its guests courtesies, facilities and conveniences that bring them back again and again... We guarantee that your stop at **The Multnomah** will be remembered as one of the very pleasant experiences of your trip. We spare no effort to preserve the reputation of this fine hotel for outstanding value and genuine hospitality.

● **FAMOUS FOODS AT POPULAR PRICES** ●

RATES

$1.50 $2.00

$2.50 $3.00

AND UP

IT COSTS NO MORE TO STOP AT THE DISTINGUISHED MULTNOMAH THAN AT ANY AVERAGE HOTEL

Fourth and Pine • Portland, Oregon

WESTERN W HOTELS INC.

Hotel Multnomah brochure from Western Hotels Inc.

father, Eric Sr. This, of course, was Portland's Multnomah Hotel. Hauser, Sr., whose ownership of the Multnomah had won him a prominent place in Portland society, had managed the hotel from 1916, when he acquired it, until his death. None of his children, who were involved in other activities, wished to undertake the Multnomah's management themselves.

The year-old hotel management company was a logical choice for the Hausers. Its member hotels, though smaller, were of the same quality as the Multnomah. The management company understood the value of the hotel's place in the Portland community as a focal point for civic and social affairs, and considered equally valuable the staff of experienced and knowledgeable managers who knew how to increase revenues and keep the hotel a profitable business for its owners.

The Multnomah
Western's Leading Asset

The Multnomah was a significant acquisition for Western for a number of reasons. It was Western's first Oregon property, and the largest. It was also a common investment by the six partners—Thurston & Maltby, the Dupars, and the Schmidts. The six, acting as Western Hotel Company, signed a contract to lease and operate the hotel, with the Hausers retaining ownership. For the first time, their theory of a centralized management group to operate independent hotels would be tested.

In 1931, the Multnomah was in desperate need of professional attention. Like so much of the industry in the United States, the hotel business had been badly hurt by the Depression, and the Multnomah was no exception. Losing over $20,000 each month, the Multnomah was draining the Hauser coffers. Despite this significant loss, the Hausers were unwilling to abandon their inheritance.

Western and the Hausers came to an agreement whereby in exchange for stock as collateral, Western would take over the entire operation of the hotel. Seeing a good investment with solid civic support and an international reputation, Western negotiated a fifteen-year lease on July 1, 1931. The company anticipated that rentals over the fifteen-year period would yield approximately $1.25 million per year.

Western immediately invested half a million dollars in remodeling. Major improvements included new bathrooms, replacement of the terrazzo floors, enclosed baths to replace the claw-footed bathtubs, and new room furnishings. The company spent $14,000 to repaint the ceiling, walls, and columns of the lobby in a fifteen-shade color scheme. Removal of the outdated pendant lights from the indirect lighting bowls left practically no direct lighting in the lobby. Western hired artists and decorators from the firms of Tourtelotte and Hummel and H. H. Clausen of Salt Lake City and employed twelve Portland painting contractors to do the work. Six weeks later, after fifteen huge Austrian loom-tufted rugs had been laid on the lobby floor (442 square yards), the renovation was complete.

To spruce up the outside, Western contracted with Electrical Products Corporation of Oregon for a 39'x156' neon sign, the largest neon sign in Oregon. The eight-foot tall letters spelling M-U-L-T-N-O-M-A-H were illuminated with a special marine green Claude neon light, the first of its kind to be seen on the Portland skyline. The marquee along the main Pine Street entrance had blue Claude neon with "Multnomah" in red.

Under Western management, the Multnomah's financial status improved immediately, bringing a nice profit to the fledgling management firm and enabling it to acquire more management contracts for hotels in Seattle, Bellingham, and Boise. The company's ability to realize a profit in the food business was instrumental in bringing all their properties, including the Multnomah, intact through the Depression. Hal Dupar's system of food-purchasing and cost-analysis for the entire chain helped keep the most expensive items of hotel operations profitable. Being the largest hotel in the chain, the Multnomah generated the most profits, and its firm management and high occupancy rates ensured a steady stream of capital for Western.

Oregon Historical Society Negative Number OrHi 96216

This large green neon sign was installed as part of the renovation of the Multnomah Hotel by Western Hotels Inc.

During the '30s and '40s profits generated by the Multnomah allowed Western to buy and lease new properties throughout the west coast, including the Benson in Portland, in which they had bought a majority ownership, and in 1941, the Sir Francis Drake in San Francisco acquired from Conrad Hilton.

E.E."Eddie" Carlson
The Whiz Kid of the Western

By 1946, the Western Hotel chain made another leap forward when it hired former bellboy Edward "Eddie" Carlson as assistant to the president, S.W. Thurston. Like his employers, the young, newly decommissioned navy commander possessed a high degree of integrity, intelligence,

and intestinal fortitude. For a starting salary of $500 per month, Carlson worked hard and displayed an intuitive sense of the direction management should take in order to ensure success. After only a few years, he was promoted from assistant to the president into the ranks of the company's executive management team where his ideas and leadership abilities helped Western become the cohesive, international, and highly competitive entity it remains to this day.

Two year after joining Western, Carlson persuaded Thurston to hold its first managers' meeting at the Multnomah. Until this time, each "house" had retained its own autonomy and the notion of a "chain" of hotels had been played down. Carlson's conviction, expressed at this meeting, that the management company, Western, should be the motivating authority persuaded Thurston, the hotel managers, and Western's Board of Directors to emphasize the company's leadership over its member properties. Soon an advertising agency was retained to "beef up" Western's image as a leading chain of the best hotel properties in the Pacific Northwest. Shaped by this image as articulated by Carlson, overall Western policies developed, solidified, and standardized operations and encouraged growth.

As a result of a sales campaign spearheaded by Carlson, Western developed and expanded first local and regional, and then national advertising over radio and in print. Western Hotel credit cards were inaugurated, and soon provided frequent business travelers a convenient means of paying their bills, especially when long trips to numerous Pacific Northwest cities encouraged putting up at Western properties.

Stirrup Room Menu

Multnomah Western Hotel brochure

Carlson's proven genius for hotel marketing brought him rapid promotions, first to the vice presidency and then to the presidency of Western from which Thurston had retired as day-to-day manager. Carlson further expanded Hal Dupar's food-service operation to include specialty room dining. Specialty rooms were dining areas found throughout the chain where the decor and even the menu highlighted a special ethnic, geographical, or sports theme. Thus, the Multnomah's Stirrup Room reflected a western theme, and both the Cafe Baron and the Golden Knight hearkened back to medieval times. The Multnomah's sister hotel, the Benson, featured Trader Vic's, which offered a Polynesian menu, drinks and decor.

©Curt Teich Postcard Archives Lake County (IL) Historical Museum

Hotel Multnomah – Portland, Oregon

The success of these innovations played no small role in Western's further expansion over the next twenty years, not only in the west but in the eastern and southern United States as well as overseas. In 1964, the Continental Plaza became the first acquisition to open up the states east of Denver. Over the years, "Western Hotels" became a synonym for gracious service in locales as near as California and Arizona and as distant as Calgary and Winnipeg, Mexico, Japan, Hong Kong, Singapore, and South Africa.

Western became international in 1970 when it was sold to United Airlines and its name changed to Westin International Hotels, Inc. "Eddie" Carlson was made president of the parent company, United Airlines, and once again demonstrated his marketing genius by leading United to become the United States' premier airline. Currently, it is an international conglomerate owned by its employees.

In the early 1980s, as the airlines were deregulated, many found themselves in financial trouble. United was no exception and divested itself of Westin, selling it to a group of American and international investors. Now independent, Westin remains a significant world-wide hotel chain based in Seattle despite the loss of most of its original properties.

A Great Success Continues

Gordon Bass, the source of much of the foregoing account, ended his story with the comment that without the Multnomah Hotel and Eddie Carlson, Western would not have gained the success it did. Even throughout the turbulent '40s and '50s the Multnomah generated over a million dollars net profit each year and supplied the financial wherewithal for Western to sustain its growth. Carlson's managerial

genius, allowing and encouraging managers to operate their houses autonomously within the framework of Western's management structure fostered stability and professionalism and resulted in a chain of first-class establishments that welcomed travelers all over the world. The Westin's continued success is a tribute not only to Carlson but to those early pioneers, Maltby and Thurston, whose classic standard—Intelligence, Integrity, Intestinal Fortitude—became the benchmark of survival in hotel management.

Courtsey of Ackroyd Photography

Fun times in the Stirrup Room

Courtesy of Washington State University Libraries

Mr. and Mrs. James Stewart during the filming of "The Bend of the River"–1952

NOTABLE GUESTS OF THE MULTNOMAH HOTEL

Lying at the northern end of the Willamette Valley on the banks of the Columbia River which separates Oregon and Washington, Portland has always been overshadowed by its larger, more cosmopolitan neighbors to the north and south–Seattle and San Francisco. But despite its retiring nature, the City of Roses has always attracted its share of the "rich and famous," men and women who for either business or pleasure come to Portland and succumb to its quiet charm. Many of the more memorable of these individuals were welcomed and served royally by the Multnomah Hotel.

"Lucky Lindy" Arrives

Flying the famous Spirit of St. Louis, the silver monoplane in which he had made his famous flight to Paris across the Atlantic Ocean, Lucky Lindy flew into Portland on a lovely fall afternoon, September 14, 1927. Halfway through a nine-month tour, America's idol, Colonel Charles A. Lindbergh had come to Portland. And Portland made no secret of its admiration for the Lone Eagle. Schools and businesses closed, state officials dropped everything, and what seemed like the entire population of Portland headed for Swan

Oregon Historical Society Negative Number OrHi 24585

Lindbergh lands "The Spirit of St. Louis" in Portland, Oregon

Island to see their hero land.

"LINDY LAND HERE" read the twenty-foot-high letters spelled out in lime on the green turf of Swan Island. Newly constructed open canvas hangars were ready near the landing site to shelter the two planes from the rain while allowing the anticipated thousands of visitors to view the famous monoplane. The day before, the Port of Portland had just finished constructing a pontoon bridge, connecting Swan Island with the mainland at Rankin Field, so that visitors could alight from buses and cars at Rankin and walk across to the island to view the plane. A temporary wooden driveway, which stretched from the southeast side of the island to the turf, provided access to the landing site for gasoline trucks and supplies and for the reception committee to approach the hero as he landed.

The rest of Portland was in readiness for Lindy. According to Superintendent C. A. Rice, the city's school children were "wild" to see the colonel. Grade and high schools had been dismissed at noon and the children instructed to head for Multnomah Stadium as fast as possible. Although Lindbergh had specified that he would speak only to the school children of Portland, parents and teachers were allowed to accompany the children. By 1:00 p.m. the stadium was filled to capacity.

The children and adults who could not get in to the stadium lined the parade route from the Battleship Oregon monument at the east end of

the Morrison Bridge north to the Burnside Bridge, and across and west on Burnside Street to the stadium. Most downtown businesses had closed their doors after lunch, including Olds, Wortman and King and Meier & Frank, two of Portland's oldest department stores. Owners Julius and Abe Meier were part of the official welcoming party for Colonel Lindbergh.

The 86th infantry band of the Oregon National Guard and the 7th Infantry band from Vancouver, Washington joined other entertainers from radio stations KOIN and KEX who provided musical and theatrical entertainment which was broadcast to those along the parade route via remote broadcast and amplified by loudspeakers.

Lindy touched down on Swan Island about 3:00 p.m. He had detoured into Portland along the Columbia River Gorge because a strong tail wind from Seattle would have made his arrival in Portland at least thirty minutes ahead of schedule. The touchdown was smooth, and after a short welcoming ceremony, the motorcade set off for the stadium. Accompanied in an open car by Mayor Baker and Governor Patterson, Lindy arrived at the stadium and was greeted by wild cheers from the crowd. The children stood at attention while the colonel and other dignitaries approached the stage and the American flag was raised. After the pledge of allegiance and an invocation and introductions by Governor Patterson and Mayor Baker, Lindy addressed the children.

Colonel Lindbergh first outlined the progress

Oregon Historical Society Negative Number CN 012440

Charles Lindbergh speaks in downtown Portland.

made by commercial aviation and its impact on their lives in the future. Describing a 16,000 mile network of airmail service that had already been developed, he stressed that this was the first commercial use made of aviation. He urged them to see to it that their "city and state were not left off the air maps" and promised that one day they themselves would be flying all over the world in airplanes. To the thousands of his young fans who had hoped to hear him tell his own adventures, it was disappointing that he did not speak of his famous flight and his plane, the Spirit of St. Louis. But Lindy had made it quite clear that this tour was not about personal accomplishments but about aviation and his job to promote it.

At the conclusion of his speech, Lindy presented awards to four young model-plane builders, winners of a contest sponsored by the *Oregon Journal* newspaper and accepted an honorary membership in Portland's Aero Club. To the three cheers of "Hip, hip hurrah," led by Mayor Baker, Lindy turned to go down the stairs of the stage to his car. Several dozen youngsters broke from their seats and ran across the field to meet him at the bottom of the stairs. Finally flashing his famous smile, Lindy saluted and said, "Hi, kids," then turned and walked to his car.

At the Multnomah all was in readiness for the late-afternoon arrival and scheduled press conference. Eric Hauser, Sr., well aware that his famous guest was the most sought-after celebrity in the world, had personally planned the formal banquet

Oregon Historical Society Negative Number OrHi 56619

Colonel Lindbergh banquet at the Multnomah Hotel on September 14, 1927

and supervised the hotel staff. Only a few rooms were needed since Lindy was flying alone, except for two others who accompanied him in the second plane. But more rooms were needed for the press and the friends and relatives Hauser had invited for the festivities. The Governor's suite was prepared for Governor Patterson, who would not return to Salem until the next day.

The Indian Grill, where the banquet was held, presented a gala scene with men and women in evening dress, an especially suitable attire for the tall, handsome, tousled-haired guest of honor. At the head table with Colonel Lindbergh were Donald Keyhoe, representative of the U.S. Department of Commerce, which was sponsoring the tour to promote commercial aviation; Philip Love, pilot of the escort plane; Governor and Mrs. Patterson; Mr. Edgar B. Piper, managing editor of *The Oregonian* newspaper, and his wife; Mayor and Mrs. George Baker, and Eric V. Hauser, Sr.

Decorated with red roses and late blooming rhododendrons, the tables were beautifully set with the Multnomah's crystal and china, the soft candlelight reflecting off the hotel's crest outlined in gold on the plates. Waiters in black trousers and white shirts served efficiently and quietly.

The dinner menu featured Toke Point oysters on the half shell, clear green turtle soup, Blue Ribbon filet mignon a la Richelieu, and an assortment of French wines. After the guests had finished, Hauser remarked that this banquet for Lindbergh was the most elaborate ever held at the Multnomah.

After a few short remarks by the mayor and governor about Lindy's flying exploits, Lindy himself rose to speak, again on his sole topic, the future of aviation. He urged further development of the radio, explaining that without adequate communication, widespread commercial air travel would be impossible and emphasizing that air-mail service would never expand until better communication existed to improve the safety of transcontinental flights. Observing that several hundred pieces of mail addressed to him had been delivered to Portland via air mail, Lindy finished his speech and, not waiting for the cheers to die down, shook hands with those at the head table, and went immediately to his room.

Along with the 500 guests at the banquet, an estimated one million radio listeners heard Lindy's speech and the entertainment broadcast live from the Indian Grill. KGW radio had installed a remote control wire arrangement to tap into its regular broadcast. Its listening public in the Portland area and far into southwest Washington and the Willamette Valley were able to participate, vicariously, in the evening's festivities.

Lindbergh remained at the Multnomah Hotel all the next day, Thursday, September 15, reading, catching up on correspondence, and preparing for the remainder of his tour. Other than greeting his former high school science teacher, Justine Dahm Jolivette, who had moved to Portland from Little Falls, Minnesota, where she had taught Lindy physics and chemistry nine years earlier, Lindy spoke to no one other than his aide Keyhoe and the hotel personnel. Hauser was able to have a cup of coffee with him Thursday evening. After a short farewell Friday morning, Lindy left the Multnomah in a small motorcade back to Swan Island and his plane.

GETTING READY FOR LINDBERGH

The Oregonian

Program cover from Elvis' 1956–57 tour

All Shook Up!

More than 14,600 screaming teenagers saw their wildest dreams come true on that hot Labor Day, September 2, 1957, when "The King," ELVIS 'THE PELVIS' PRESLEY, CAME TO TOWN!

The Elvis phenomenon began about 1955, when the young, handsome, country- and gospel-singer from Memphis first hit the charts with such new style "pop" tunes as "Hound Dog" and "All Shook Up." Adult America shuddered at the long, highly oiled ducktail haircut and the lower body "wiggle" that appeared—well, indecent. But the younger generation admired his style, his beat, and unique style of clothing. Stunned that their idol was coming to town, many Portland teenagers worked long hours to earn the five dollar admission fee and an extra few dollars for souvenirs.

Portland knew it had never seen anything like Elvis and probably never would again. When approached for reservations, the Multnomah Hotel was brave enough to accommodate the icon and his entourage despite the heavy security needed and the difficulty in providing "The King" with the privacy for which the Multnomah was famous.

It was difficult, but exciting, acknowledged Bill Williams, assistant manager at the time. Elvis, his manager, the already infamous Colonel Tom Parker, and a dozen other members of the party arrived on Monday, from where, no one was quite sure It was routine for the Multnomah to ferry guests' baggage and equipment from the airport or the train depot, but Parker, known for his tough negotiating style and fierce protection of his client, declined all such assistance. In fact, it was only a few days before Monday's arrival that he had informed the Multnomah that the Presley party would be staying at the hotel. It was later learned that Elvis and his party had arrived by private plane late Monday morning.

An advance list of requirements for "The King" had included no indication of how many rooms would be needed. So Bill Williams had several of the 7th floor suites prepared, knowing that they could be used separately or opened up to make a four- or six-room lounging area. The pantries were stocked with peanut butter, bananas, white bread, grits (not usually available in Portland), and bottles and bottles of Coke, Elvis' favorite soft drink. Cooks stood ready to fry pork chops, make brown gravy and bake fresh apple pies at any hour of the day or night. The housekeeping staff made sure that new, freshly washed and ironed linens were on the beds, and thick towels were hanging in the bathrooms. It was rumored that a housekeeper could make a fortune by smuggling "The King's" sheets out of the hotel and into the hands of souvenir buyers who would cut them up into one-inch squares and sell them to fans. But to their credit, not one employee violated the Multnomah's reputation for discreet service and protective care of all guests, famous or not.

By 8:00 o'clock Monday morning, just twelve hours before the concert of the century was to begin, all was ready. Anxiously, the staff kept watch for the party. The extra security men, fidgeting as they waited, occasionally ushered fans who had somehow made it into the lobby out again. The younger bellmen rushed to finish any task that took them away from the lobby for even a minute. Finally, in early afternoon, Elvis' advance men arrived at the hotel and announced that Elvis was in town. They signed the party in, but gave no indication when Elvis would be arriving. Even Frank Breall, the local Portland jeweler and impresario who had booked the act, was uncertain about Elvis' whereabouts.

When Elvis finally arrived, Bill Williams was impressed with his quiet air, apparent kindness, and lack of ego. Presley went out of his way to sign autographs, shake hands, and make small talk with the staff and those guests lucky enough to be in the vicinity. Despite heavy security, some fans, mostly teenage girls, kept vigils outside and did their best to get near their idol. One enterprising young lady was caught scaling the Pine Street facade in an attempt to get into a second-floor window. Close to success, she was hauled down before she could reach the window.

Elvis spent the afternoon in his suite, emerging only about 7:00 p.m., dressed casually in slacks, open shirt and jacket, and headed out for the Multnomah Athletic Club, adjacent to the Multnomah stadium where he was to perform. For over an hour, Elvis held a press conference and interview with members of the local press, teen representatives of several high schools and fan clubs, and fans

The Oregonian

Newspaper ad with Elvis memorabilia offered for sale

lucky enough to know somebody to get them in. He graciously answered questions about a steady girlfriend (he had none at the time), the draft (he was ready to go when called, and felt it a privilege to serve his country), and numerous other subjects the press and fans wanted to know about him. Finally, just before 8:30 p.m., when the concert was scheduled to begin, he ended the interviews.

Opening for Elvis that night were a number of local comedians and music groups that barely held the fans' attention. After them, came The Jordanaires, whose national reputation and hit songs were more familiar to the young crowd. Finally, after a short intermission and a few more acts, around 10:00 p.m., with the tension so high it was electric, Elvis made his appearance in his trademark open convertible, dressed in a black shirt, tight black trousers, and blue satin jacket. The approving roar from the crowd was so loud that one fan believed it could be heard "all the way to Memphis"!

Another roar rose from 14,000 throats as "The King" sang the first note of his opening song, "Heartbreak Hotel," accompanied by The Jordanaires. Amid all the screams and clapping, the crowd heard almost an hour of music. A few girls fainted from the excitement and had to be carried out, but Portland's well-behaved crowd did not rush the stage, as other crowds in other places had done, and the night ended with everyone exhausted but happy.

Elvis returned to the Multnomah for a late dinner, which he ate in his suite with Colonel Parker and others. By Tuesday evening, Elvis had left, the excitement was over, and all was back to normal. He had impressed not only his paying fans, but those who had met him and received his polite and courteous attention.

Elvis never returned to Portland. But there are still many Portlanders, now grandparents, who treasure the souvenir programs pasted into their scrapbooks, waiting to tell their grandchildren about the time they saw Elvis!

Presidential Politics

During its 53-year history, the Multnomah Hotel was fortunate to have as guests such notable presidents as Theodore Roosevelt, Warren G. Harding, Herbert Hoover, Franklin D. Roosevelt, Harry S. Truman, Dwight D. Eisenhower, John F. Kennedy, Lyndon B. Johnson, and Richard M. Nixon. Most came to Portland and the Northwest on campaign trips or, in Roosevelt's case, to dedicate Bonneville Dam and Timberline Lodge. Many of their political rivals, such as Thomas Dewey, Harold Stassen, Adlai Stevenson, Hubert Humphrey, and Barry Goldwater, as well as several congressmen and women also were guests at the Multnomah Hotel. Their presence attested to the growing importance even this sparsely populated state had and continues to have on national elections.

A Visit Cut Short

Timberline Lodge hunkers down at the tree line of Oregon's Mt. Hood. Built by the Civilian Conservation Corps (CCC) in 1936, the beautiful log structure attests to the craftsmanship of the hundreds of workers who labored on it. Hand-finished native Douglas fir floors and furniture, a massive fireplace constructed with stones hauled down from the slopes of Mt. Hood, and hand-woven Native American wall decorations are among the features that make it one of the most unique projects ever completed by the corps.

President Franklin D. Roosevelt arrived in Portland on a cold day in February, 1936, to dedicate the lodge. Under cloudy, gray skies, with the temperature in the low 40s, Portland was experiencing its usual winter weather, which surprised the president

© Jon Tullis, Timberline Lodge

Timberline Lodge and Mount Hood

who seemed to think that it should have been warm, like southern California!

The trip to Mt. Hood, some fifty miles up the Columbia River gorge to the east, began soon after the president arrived in Portland. The schedule called for the president to travel to Timberline, dedicate the building, have a late lunch, and then return to stay overnight at the Multnomah Hotel. Gordon Bass and Hal Carey, assistant managers at the hotel, were to accompany the presidential party and play a minor role in the dedication. Earl McInnes, the Multnomah's manager, had volunteered to supply the lodge temporarily with kitchen equipment since the lodge lacked its own. Knowing that the small kitchen off the Rose Bowl was used infrequently, McInnes had earlier directed that all of its equipment be shipped up to Timberline in time for the dedication. Along with a kitchen crew, Bass and Carey were to oversee the preparation of the presidential meal. Hot dogs and sodas could be purchased by those spectators not fortunate enough to be invited for lunch.

Oregon Historical Society Negative Number CN 019627

Governor Charles Sprague, H. J. Kaiser, Edgar Kaiser, and F. D. R. in 1942

As the party made its way east on Burnside Road, it became apparent past the small town of Sandy that snow could be expected momentarily. Nevertheless, the party decided to push on to Timberline. Hardly had the dedication begun, however, when down came the snow in big, wet flakes that soon covered the cars and spectators with a thick blanket, a portent of more to come.

Deciding that it would not do for the leader of the free world to be snowbound in some freezing corner of Oregon with minimal communications capabilities, the president's aides, ever mindful of their chief's national and global responsibilities, advised Mr. Roosevelt to keep his remarks short and to skip lunch. He took their advice, and within the hour, his car and those of the other dignitaries were headed down the mountain as fast as they could safely travel.

Left behind, Bass and Carey saw no reason to hook up the kitchen for a guest who had already left, but they were aware that there were a number of very hungry people wanting something to eat. So they passed out cold hot dogs and icy sodas, and remained "stuck" at the beautiful new lodge for the next couple of days. As Hal Carey later remarked: "It's not every day that unforeseen circumstances (like a snowstorm) prevent a hotel man from attending to his duties."

"We Like Ike!"

Dwight D. Eisenhower was the only president who stayed overnight at the Multnomah while in office. In October, 1958, Eisenhower was struggling for reelection against Adlai Stevenson and was making sure he did not miss any opportunity to reach staunch Republicans. The president's visit was scheduled less than a month before the election. Accompanied by his wife, Mamie, Ike was to stay overnight in Portland before going on to Los Angeles.

Only moments before the Columbine III landed at Portland airport at 2:00 p.m. Thursday, October 18, the heavens had opened and several hundred press corps and a handful of Oregon Republican dignitaries waiting for the president got soaked. But just as President and Mrs. Eisenhower deplaned, the rain eased up, and a shout of welcome arose from the crowd. Striding down the steps and over to the waiting dignitaries, Eisenhower shook hands with Douglas McKay, who had left Ike's cabinet to run for the United States Senate, and greeted him with the words, "Doug, my boy, how are you doing?" He then greeted Mrs. McKay, Governor and Mrs. Elmo Smith, Mayor and Mrs. Fred Peterson, and State Senator Mark Hatfield among others on the platform.

President Eisenhower speaking at Portland's Civic Auditorium in October, 1956.

Oregon Historical Society Negative Number Or Hi 0334 A191

McKay introduced Ike to the crowd and to the chant of "We like Ike," the President replied, "I like you, too." He then remarked on what a fine senator McKay would make. As the rain began again, the party headed under umbrellas to the waiting cars. The parade into Portland was quick, the president standing outside the bubble dome in the rain and Mrs. Eisenhower sheltering under its half-open Plexiglas. Through the streets of the Hollywood District and across the Burnside Bridge, the motorcade made its way past crowds estimated at 100,000 or more to Portland's Civic Auditorium at 3rd and Clay Streets.

At the auditorium, the president gave a short speech, reiterating the successes of his first administration and noting that "people look better off than they were four years ago." The packed crowd of journalists and Portland leaders clapped and cheered, and at the conclusion of his speech the party returned to the motorcade to make the short trip to the Multnomah Hotel.

Courtesy of Washington State University Libraries

President Dwight and Mamie Eisenhower with Multnomah Hotel Manager C. R. Lindquist (left) upon their arrival at the Fourth Street entrance.

At the Multnomah, Manager Bob Lindquist had supervised the total renovation of the Presidential Suite. Both *The Oregonian* and *The Oregon Journal* ran pictures of the suite, giving every detail of the furniture and the decorations.

The rooms were decorated with new wallpaper, paint, and pictures, mostly flower prints. The carpet, a lovely shade of autumn red, was new, and the twin beds in the master bedroom were covered with matching maroon spreads. Easy chairs and writing desks completed the furnishings, except for the television. The Multnomah had only recently furnished its suites with the black and white sets that were becoming more and more common. Knowing that the paint had dried only hours before, Lindquist hoped that the president and his wife would not be overcome by the smell of fresh paint.

Lindquist had reserved the entire east side of the seventh floor, including two bedrooms, a dining/sitting room, and two bathrooms for the first couple. Other rooms could be used for socializing or as offices for the Secret Service men accompanying the president. Each phone in the suite was labeled, "Multnomah White House No. 1, 2," etc. Lindquist even saw to it that there was a phone in each bathroom.

When the Eisenhowers arrived at the Multnomah about 4:30 that afternoon, Lindquist received them at the Fourth Street entrance which had become the new main entrance to the hotel. Escorting the president and his wife, the McKays, and the governor and his wife to the elevator reserved for their exclusive use, Lindquist showed them to their suites where they asked to have an early dinner before they were driven back to the auditorium for an 8:00 o'clock speech. Before sitting down to dinner, the president had asked Bellman Sammy Miller to serve drinks to the party. When he rang for a second scotch, Miller heard him ask Mamie if it was all right for him to have another. She gave her permission, and Sammy brought the scotch and a dry martini for Mamie. The first couple then dined alone: a pot roast-potatoes-and-vegetable dinner with coffee and fresh pie, after which they returned to the auditorium.

The Multnomah had made preparations to accomodate the White House Press Corps of 65 reporters and correspondents, many of whom remarked to Lindquist that they had never been

Oregon Historical Society Negative Number Or Hi 72866

President Eisenhower's bedroom suite

In preparation for the Eisenhower visit, the staff at the Multnomah Hotel totally renovated the Presidential suite.

Oregon Historical Society

President Eisenhower's sitting room

treated so well. Lindquist had installed telephones and teletype machines for their use in one of the junior ballrooms. The reporters, accustomed to long waits at pay phones to call in their stories to their newspapers were audibly grateful. The hotel had also arranged to accommodate the heavy lights and equipment of the television reporters. Lindquist had also ordered a bountiful smorgasbord and a well-equipped bar for the press. Having just come from Seattle and Olympia, where coffee and sandwiches were the only refreshments offered, the reporters and technicians were overjoyed at the Multnomah's brand of hospitality. Lindquist knew that the Multnomah's fame would be spread far and wide by the grateful reporters.

The last activity of the long day was a press conference called by Press Secretary Hagerty after the president had gone to bed. There were many questions about the president's earlier speeches, but (as *The Oregonian* recounted) foremost was the question: Why do we have to be ready to leave at 7:00 the next morning when the president is not due to arrive in Los Angeles until the evening? Acknowledging that he had no answer to that, Hagerty wished them all a good night.

Early the next morning, all was in readiness for the president, who routinely rose at 5:00 o'clock. The first couple was served a big farm breakfast in their room, and after signing a few autographs and waving to the crowds lining the lobby, took their leave of the Multnomah and Portland.

Brothers in Arms

One of the most poignant moments in the Multnomah's history occurred in the Spring of 1960, when John F. Kennedy and his brother, Robert, were in Portland on a final western campaign swing before the fall election. Kennedy made the Multnomah his headquarters for the few days he was in the state, and although he was seldom in residence, the entire building was infused with the energetic, happy spirit of this engaging, handsome senator, who looked too young to be running for the presidency of the United States. People were drawn to his shy grin, his jokes about the rain in an accent so broad that many native Oregonians had trouble deciphering it, and one could almost see their transformation from polite strangers to whole-hearted supporters after only a few direct words from the senator.

As Bill Williams remembers it, Jack and Robert Kennedy walked into the Multnomah lobby fairly late one evening, around 10:00 o'clock. Returning from a political dinner, they were deep in conversation. No security or aides accompanied them: just the two brothers, whose mutual affection was evident in their gestures and rapport. Asking a passing bellman to bring them a drink, the two men, obviously tired, continued their conversation as they walked up the stairs to the balcony. Here they stood for some minutes oblivious to the still rather considerable traffic in the lobby.

Observing the scene from a discreet distance, Williams was struck by the strong, magnetic pull that seemed to emanate from the two. This "pull" was apparent not only to him but to the stragglers in the lobby as well for they soon gathered below the balcony and observed the brothers in silence. Finally, Jack became aware of the people below. Interrupting his brother, he flashed a smile and waved to the crowd. When a few of the more outgoing began to shout up questions to him, Kennedy shrugged his shoulders and began to speak. For about ten minutes, he regaled the crowd with his hopes for the future and for what, working together, the people of America could accomplish. Unrehearsed and unpolished, the message was nevertheless, clear, strong, and persuasive. His listeners never forgot the dreams of the young man whose enthusiasm for and love for his country and the world would usher in a new wave of patriotism in only three short years.

No camera was available to catch some of the magic of the scene, but Bill Williams will never forget the image of the two brothers standing side-by-side on the balcony of the Multnomah Hotel.

UPI/Corbis-Bettmann

Attorney General Robert F. Kennedy and President John F. Kennedy in conversation at the White House.

Oreogn Historical Society Negative Number MSS1510

Dining room menu

The hotel's own print shop made it possible to change menus frequently.

Hal Carey Collection

Hotel Personalities bulletin board
Honoring Hal Carey's sports prowess
(Hans Rampmeier on the left, Hal Carey on the right)

ALL-TIME FAVORITE STORIES ABOUT THE MULTNOMAH

Many of the Multnomah's long-time former employees have proved to be a storehouse of anecdotes and stories about the events and persons who visited the Multnomah over the years. Their memories, which go as far back as 1935 and even earlier, have become part of Portland's folklore, tales that will live on as long as the "Grand Lady" stands.

Some of these vignettes are related in the following pages. The compiler's hope is that the reader will derive as much pleasure in their recounting as the Multnomah family did in the actual events.

It Pays to be Thrifty

Eddie Carlson and Gordon Bass were always looking for ways to save money. Bass recalled two particularly novel ways the hotel staff were instructed to be thrifty. The staff were ordered to always walk at the edge of the carpeting close to the walls of the corridors and rooms. This instruction not only saved wear and tear on the main section of the carpet, but also allowed guests the right-of-way down the center of the hallways. As a result of this

economy, the Multnomah's carpets lasted two or three years longer than expected.

Soon after arriving at the Multnomah in 1935, Bass noticed a pitcher of cream standing on every table in the dining room. Very soon, the pitchers were removed from the tables and cream was served only when a guest expressly asked for it!

Performance Dining
The "Baron of Beef" Leads the Way

The Multnomah was probably the first hotel in Portland to provide what we might call today "Performance Dining." Beginning in 1912, H. C. Bowers, the Multnomah's first manager, introduced vaudeville acts in the Arcadian Garden. Soon he added live orchestral music and concerts for guests and the general public. These, and musical and theatrical performances, always remained a part of the dining experience at the Multnomah.

The tradition continued until 1931 when the Western Hotel chain assumed management of the Multnomah. At that time they introduced "theme" dining establishments in the hotel. One of the first was the Cafe Baron, located in the main lobby near the Fourth Street entrance. Furnished in the style of a medieval dining hall, the Cafe Baron featured an ordinary roast of beef as its main attraction. Using a recent innovation, the hotel's chef placed the large cut of meat under infra-red warming lights that kept the meat warm without drying it out. This warming tray was strategically placed near the main entrance to the Cafe Baron so that patrons would be enticed by the succulent, juicy roast to enter and order.

The strategy worked, so Bass decided to add an extra touch of glamour. In honor of the cafe, he renamed the roast "Baron of Beef" and at 5:00 p.m. each day, had four waiters, dressed in page-boy outfits parade around the lobby with the Baron of Beef on a litter carried on their shoulders and accompanied by trumpets heralding the arrival of the famous "Baron"!

When Bass ascertained from dozens of meat packers throughout the country that this particular cut had never been called by any other name, he claimed the "Baron of Beef" as Multnomah's own. Soon the name and fame of the roast spread throughout the Western Hotel chain, not only in the United States but in Mexico, Puerto Rico, and Europe.

Later, the Cafe Baron was remodeled and renamed the Golden Knight. A suit of armor—the knight—at the entrance to the room acted as a drawing card. The "knight" greeted favored guests by name and wished them a pleasant evening! Businessmen trying to impress their clients or bosses were assured that their guests would be pleased by this special attention. A phone call to the "knight" some hours before the scheduled dinner to relay the guests' names always ensured his cooperation!

The 1960 season's opening of the Golden Knight continued the Multnomah's tradition of performance dining. In fact, every meal in this medieval banquet hall became a stellar performance. Pairs of

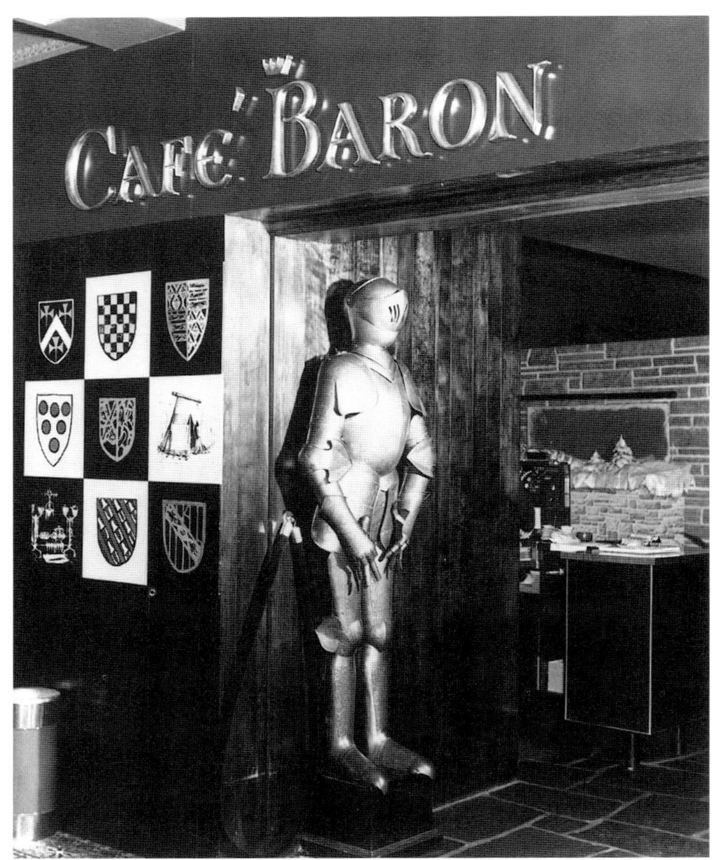

Photo by Al Monner
Oregon Historical Society Negative Number Or Hi 96217

Where the world-famous "Baron of Beef" was introduced in 1932

Courtesy of Ackroyd Photography
Performance dining at the Golden Knight in 1962
Until the hotel closed, the Golden Knight staff referred to themselves as the "Jolly Jesters."

waitresses in tunics and tights and twirling flaming batons of lamb skewers greeted the lamb-lovers. Those who ordered the Golden Champagne dinner were approached by waitresses balancing rows of narrow-stemmed champagne glasses (filled) on the backs of their hands. Some of the more talented performers even skipped while balancing the glasses! Such elaborate entertainment presaged an eventful meal involving the entire dining room.

The novelty of performance dining attracted the wealthy and curious, and with them, large amounts of money to the Multnomah as well as to the other hotels in the Western chain. Proof of its profitability was the fact that from the very first day, the hotel's restaurant ledger showed black. Hotel employees attributed the rising profits to not only the Golden Champagne dinners but also the Jester section, a drinking room, or bar, that featured mid-day pick-me-ups for the downtown business crowd and the luncheon-meeting crowd that filled the Multnomah each working day.

The Multnomah was a steady provider of inspiration for Doug Baker, Portland's preeminent newspaper columnist, who wrote a daily column, "Baker's Dozen," for the *Oregon Journal*. In the May 4, 1961, column, Baker regaled his readers with the following anecdotes about the Multnomah:

> Fancy names for cocktail bars have become so common that the Multnomah's Ken Kinney has just named his simply, "The Drinking Room." This takes some of the guests a little aback, even though the sign is faced with $20 worth of gold leaf.
>
> Newest acquisition at the Golden Knight is a round, solid-oak table which belonged to Herbert B. Cooper, the lumberman, until the hotel bought it for businessmen's round table luncheons. If you're going to be drunk under the table, pick a good solid one, I always say.
>
> Finally, Baker concludes:
>
> In my anecdotage about the hotel, I mustn't forget to tell you that they have a unique ball viol player. She's Aloma Mayor who strums Russian gypsy melodies, Viennese waltzes and other listenable schmaltz. So what? So she does all this while wearing a pair of black gloves.

To this day, no one knows why the lady bass strummer played with her gloves on, but it was good for a story in the newspaper and for the Multnomah's coffers!

Occasionally, guests and staff of the Multnomah would receive an unexpected treat, an impromptu performance by a professional entertainer staying at the hotel. Once during the '50s, Patti Page, America's Sweetheart Singer, serenaded the lobby guests and front-desk staff with a medley of her most popular tunes. Margaret Whiting, another singer and contemporary of Judy Garland from

the '40s, once gave a private recital to Hal Carey as he was stowing her luggage in her suite!

Dinner theater was as popular as musical entertainment at the Multnomah. The Rose Bowl in the lower level hosted many local semi-professional and amateur theater productions and this helped give Portland its reputation for live theater. The Jewish Community Theater, Portland State College, and the University of Portland held productions at the hotel and many a Portland actor has fond memories of playing to the crowd at the Multnomah.

Benny's Ball

The management of the Multnomah were always amenable to helping Portland's non-profit associations raise money for their activities. One favorite organization was the Portland Symphony. With the symphony's board of directors, and the help of the Westin's Benson Hotel, the Multnomah held two of the most fun and innovative events the city had ever experienced.

The first of these was the Portland Symphony Gala, "Manhattan West." Over two days, the Multnomah and the Benson hosted a series of events that drew on the popularity of New York City theater and its note-worthy night clubs. To start the fund-raising, the hotels sponsored "The College Premier," on Friday, February 1, 1963. An evening of fun and dancing with a college theme, "The College Premier" featured musical theater entertainment performed by local college students. Saturday afternoon found Portland's most sophisticated ladies attending the "Critic's Choice," a fashion show of fabulous gowns by America's leading designers. From 11 o'clock until 3 o'clock in the afternoon, the ladies who would attend the ball later that night could view New York's haute couture fashion designs and, if lucky, find a new ball gown for that evening!

A scant four hours later, fourteen rooms in the Multnomah and Benson hotels were transformed into famous Manhattan night clubs: "Club 21," "Sardi's," "The Rainbow Room," and "Delmonico's," among others. This one-of-a-kind fund-raiser was fabulous, with each "night club" an exact replica of its famous counterpart in New York. The organizers asked for, and received from, the New York clubs many of the accouterments of the famous rooms, including napkins and matchbooks embossed with the club name, swizzle sticks, and coat check tags. Patrons, paying $25 per couple, spent the evening moving from room to room in each hotel and then walking the four blocks to the other. There was live music in each "club," and the region's most famous entertainers put on performances that rivaled those found in Manhattan.

The Symphony Gala was such a success in 1963 that it was repeated in a slightly different manner the next year. The symphony invited the well-loved Jack Benny to perform with it on November 8, 1964. The Multnomah volunteered to sponsor "Benny's Ball" the night before, and symphony volunteers and hotel staff decorated the grand ball room and the junior ball rooms in Benny's familiar themes. Each room was sponsored by friends of the symphony, and again guests moved from room to room, sampling all the entertainment for which

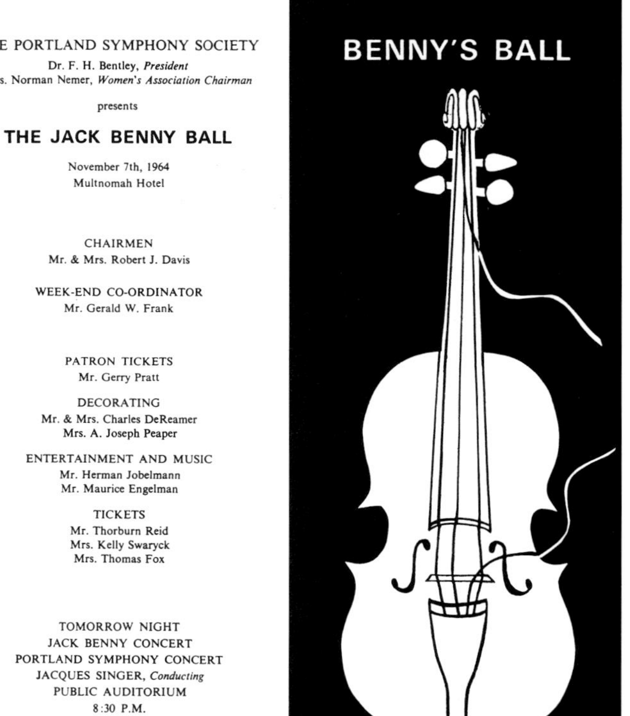

THE PORTLAND SYMPHONY SOCIETY
Dr. F. H. Bentley, *President*
Mrs. Norman Nemer, *Women's Association Chairman*

presents

THE JACK BENNY BALL

November 7th, 1964
Multnomah Hotel

CHAIRMEN
Mr. & Mrs. Robert J. Davis

WEEK-END CO-ORDINATOR
Mr. Gerald W. Frank

PATRON TICKETS
Mr. Gerry Pratt

DECORATING
Mr. & Mrs. Charles DeReamer
Mrs. A. Joseph Peaper

ENTERTAINMENT AND MUSIC
Mr. Herman Jobelmann
Mr. Maurice Engelman

TICKETS
Mr. Thorburn Reid
Mrs. Kelly Swaryck
Mrs. Thomas Fox

TOMORROW NIGHT
JACK BENNY CONCERT
PORTLAND SYMPHONY CONCERT
JACQUES SINGER, *Conducting*
PUBLIC AUDITORIUM
8:30 P.M.

BENNY'S BALL

Portland Symphony Society's Benny's Ball at the Multnomah Hotel, Noveber 7, 1964

Benny was famous: comedy and music, jokes and scratchy violins!

Portland's non-profits loved to hold their fundraisers in the Multnomah. While not all of them matched the gala spectaculars of the symphony, the Multnomah always could be counted on to make each event a special and profitable one for the organization.

Marooned at the Multnomah

During the winter of 1960, dinner theater took on a new significance. Snow reached to the top of the trees in front of the Multnomah and was so deep that Tom Gowman, manager, ordered that a temporary Fourth Street entrance be made out of one of the windows in Room 212! As a hotel account recorded: ". . . hundreds of Portlanders were marooned [downtown] and they all came to the Multnomah. They swarmed in like frivolous lemmings, and the gaiety that ensued was enough to make us remember it forever."

With occupancy well over a hundred percent, the hotel's lobby and restaurants were filled to capacity with loud, boisterous citizens making the most of a natural catastrophe. Sing-alongs in one room added to the din of impromptu recitations and hilarious skits in adjoining rooms, and made for a memorable night at the Multnomah! To this day, stories about being "Marooned at the Multnomah" in 1960 can be heard!

For a Good Time Call . . . CApitol 8-7441

Always a convivial place, the Multnomah catered to conventioneers and Portlanders out for a good time. In the days before concern about the hazards of drinking and driving put a damper on them, restaurants and bars did a thriving business pushing "Happy Hours" and other novelties designed to lure people in to drink and eat. The Multnomah was a leader at this being the first hotel in Oregon to serve liquor by the glass. As soon as the ban (a holdover from Prohibition) against the purchase of a single drink was lifted in 1954, Bill Keithan, Western's catering expert, was transferred to the Multnomah precisely to inaugurate the Multnomah's bar and to help the staff market this novel and welcome idea. He chose the beautiful Rose Bowl room on the lower level to begin serving liquor. Its old-fashioned, elegant setting enhanced the enjoyment of the formally attired guests enjoying exotic cocktails and dining to the strains of Bart Woodrow or Jack Baine!

The Multnomah was always ready to hold promotional events that revolved around its food and beverage menus. For many years each fall, the Multnomah had been the headquarters hotel for the annual football games played by the rival University of Oregon and Oregon State, and University of Oregon and University of Washington, at the Multnomah Stadium, a short walk from the hotel. Many of the schools' alumni spent rowdy weekends at the Multnomah. Hal Carey remembers (with shudders!) that some alums, already well oiled, once erected goal posts in the lobby and had a contest to see how many could kick the football from one end of the lobby, through the goal posts, up on to the balcony. This event added another dimension to the normal party atmosphere in the lobby: pennants, pom-poms, beanies, and other college memorabilia were everywhere. Portable bars and hot-dog stands provided sustenance and ensured that the alumni had every opportunity to revive their old collegiate spirit! Ever solicitous, the Multnomah provided buses to transport guests safely to and from the stadium.

The alumni parties each fall at the Multnomah "inspired" another popular event one year (1962). Always on the lookout for an opportunity to make one's stay at the hotel memorable, Bob Kennedy, the zany, balding director of public relations at the Multnomah, acquired a golf cart, gathered up some basic medical equipment, and had the printing shop make a sign: Olds-plasma-Mobile. Clad in a white coat, "Doctor" Bob, medicine case and i.v. needle in hand, loaded the storage compartment of the Plasma Mobile with ice and the "makings." Sunday morning (not too early!), the day after the Big Game, he toured the floors of the hotel, bringing "first aid" to

guests suffering with that old ailment, "Morning Afteritis." As the hotel's newsletter recounted, "Just as the historic St. Bernard dogs brought life-restoring fluid to stranded mountain climbers in the Swiss Alps, faithful 'Dr. Bob' brought restoring plasma (Bloody Marys) to hotel guests on the upper slopes of the Multnomah. The venture was a 'smash' hit and as the Plasma Mobile passed up and down the hallways, there were cries of 'We're next,' or 'Take some to our friends in Room 878.' " Kennedy and the hotel made a great many friends and some money. As for the Washington fans, it gave them something to talk about on the way home besides how they had lost the game!

Good times at the Multnomah were not always public. When discretion was needed, staff could be counted on to be discreet. Each guest room door had a transom which could be opened and shut by the occupants. Bill Williams remembers that many times the front desk would receive complaints that occupants of an adjoining room were making too much noise. It was his delicate task to go up and quietly interrupt the guests' private entertainment and ask them to close the transom!

For years, the girlfriend of one of Portland's most respected citizens lived at the Multnomah, where her paramour was a frequent guest. Each month, Mr. X would pay for the lady's suite, registered under the name, "Bud Smith." Although the staff knew Mr. X was "Bud Smith," they never revealed the connection and kept his secret as long as the couple held their trysts at the Multnomah.

Occasionally, a death would occur at the hotel. Once, a guest had not been seen for a day or two, and his messages were piling up in his box. After a particularly distraught call from his wife, the hotel manager decided to open the room to ascertain the whereabouts of the guest. There, sitting on the commode, was the guest–dead!

Another visitor did not die alone at the Multnomah. One afternoon, one of Portland's finest was engaged in a rendezvous with his lady friend at the Multnomah. Suddenly she called down in hysterics to the front desk. Evidently, the stress had proved too much for his heart and he had expired, naked, upon the bed. The hotel staff dressed the body and laid it out in the room in which all evidence of the lady's presence had been removed. They then telephoned the man's wife and told her that, unfortunately, he had taken ill and died while lunching at the hotel.

Portland's Civic Center

The Multnomah was not only a comfortable place to stay and be entertained, it was also a focal point for community events, including political and charitable fund-raisers, business and political discussions, and civic affairs. Many of these events provided stories about people and the hotel that are still remembered.

Portlander Walt Gadsby remembers that the Multnomah was the site of the first "Bundles for Britain" fundraising rummage sale in 1939. All across the United States, volunteers ran these sales throught the war years in order to support America's British Allies. Gadsby, 20 years old at the time, recalls that his father bought him a brand-new Smith Corona typewriter at that sale. It was young Gadsby's first reality of war.

Because so much of Portland's business was conducted at the Multnomah, it became the place to ferret out what was happening in town. During the '50s, Portland's most visible news reporters on radio and television–Tom McCall, Richard Ross and Ivan Smith–would interview prominent political figures and entertainment celebrities who would invariably be staying at the Multnomah. Sometimes, these interviews would last throughout a meal. For Tom McCall, at least, the politicians with whom he spoke were always interesting and informative. McCall would later become Oregon's beloved governor, a giant not only in stature but in his efforts for conservation. His exposure to national and international visitors to the state began during his days as a reporter. The time he spent at the Multnomah Hotel enabled him to develop and debate his political views on local, regional, and national issues with some of the nation's highest political figures.

As reporter, candidate, and governor, McCall met many local and national politicians at the Multnomah. All of Oregon's late-20th century political giants–Senator Wayne Morse, Senator Edith Green,

Oregon Historical Society Negative Number CN 012491
Tom McCall during a session of his "Viewpoint" program

Governor (and then Senator) Mark Hatfield, Senators Richard and Maurine Neuburger—found their way to the Multnomah whenever they were in Portland. Senator Hatfield (who was Oregon's governor after McCall) spent his wedding night at the Multnomah.

Many of the city's social and service clubs also used the Multnomah Hotel as their base, holding meetings, luncheons, and social affairs in its brilliant lobby and graceful banquet rooms. For years Portland's Rose Festival Association made their headquarters at the Multnomah, using space donated by Eric Hauser on the mezzanine and second floor. During the festival itself in June, the Multnomah hosted the queen's coronation and allowed the court's personal cars, one for the queen and one each for the princesses, to be driven into the lobby to pick up the royalty and take them to their float at the beginning of the parade route.

The Associated General Contractors not only held their meetings at the Multnomah but reserved office space there for almost three decades. The Propeller Club and the Advertising Club of Portland held their meetings at the Multnomah. The former included representatives of Portland's extensive

shipping industry; since many of the shipping lines had their offices in the Multnomah (Matson Steamship Lines, Hawaii Steamship Lines, etc.), it was a natural meeting place.

Hugh Ackroyd, local Portland photographer for over 50 years, recalls the days when the clubs would meet over lunch. Sometimes the lunch hour would extend into the afternoon when a Multnomah manager or two would join the members. Ackroyd was often invited for cocktails and dinner with hotel managers, Earl McInnes and Gordon Bass. Once, after a particularly jovial meal, they signed their tabs, using the names of the Western Hotels International (WHI) officers! There was hell to pay for that one, Ackroyd relates. After that, the staff was instructed to make sure they examined the tabs very carefully! One WHI official was always good for drinks and dinner, but as the evening wore on, his writing got worse and worse until his signature on the tab became illegible. The hotel solved that problem by making up a rubber stamp of his signature which he used from then on.

It was customary for the hotel executives to meet at 5:00 o'clock in the evening to review the day just past and the day ahead. These meetings could go on for some time, and one retired manager related that if he wanted to get home in one piece afterwards (as expected by his wife), he would give orders privately to the barman to substitute soda for gin in his drink!

During the presidential election year of 1948, Thomas Dewey, New York's governor and Harold E. Stassen, ex-governor of Minnesota, were engaged in a battle for the Republican nomination. The two candidates were in Oregon for a full two weeks during May. In Portland, Stassen stayed at the Imperial and Dewey at the Multnomah, where they were scheduled to debate the issue, "Shall the Communist Party be Outlawed?" in an hour-long, nationwide radio broadcast. After the debate was over and Dewey and Stassen moved on, Hugh Ackroyd relates that he and Frank Womack, president of the Portland Chamber of Commerce, persuaded the management to give them the key to the presidential suite, which Dewey had occupied. Just in case they could say later that November that they had "bathed where 'President' Dewey had bathed," the two men took turns taking a bath in the Presidential Suite's bathtub!

These stories, as related by those close to the Multnomah during its 53-year history, capture the spirit and flavor of this important part of Portland's history and illustrate the kind of place Portland was, and continues to be: warm and welcoming. The Multnomah and Portland allowed guests and citizens, the famous and infamous, to catch a glimpse of life outside the bounds of their own existence and to participate in events that brought smiles to their faces and laughter to their lips. But above all, it enabled them to experience the best of what Portland had to offer while still being able to remain themselves. Many individuals have recalled their experiences at the Multnomah. For most, they have lasted a lifetime.

Photo by Maurice Hodge, Courtesy of the Hal Carey Collection

The Bellmen—circa 1930

THE GRAND LADY RETIRES

The retirement of the Multnomah as a working hotel came slowly. In 1958, Western began negotiating with the Hauser Estate to obtain a renewal of its operating lease on the hotel. Anticipating a twenty-year extension, Edward "Eddie" Carlson, Western's chairman, scheduled a one-million-dollar remodeling project to begin as soon as the lease was signed. The remodeling included new elevators and extensive renovations to all the public and guest rooms. At the same time, Carlson announced that Western would raze the old Oregon Hotel building to accommodate a three-million-dollar extension to the Benson, the Multnomah's sister hotel in which Western owned an interest. Although Carlson made it clear that this major investment signified Western's confidence in the hotel industry and in Portland, privately he was worried about a stagnant growth rate in the region and some coming competition in the city itself.

At least one new hotel was being planned for Portland's downtown district. A group of local investors had access to a site a few blocks south of the Multnomah. Meeting with the city council, they

explored the possibility of the city granting them tax credits and other financial incentives in exchange for the employment opportunities and revenues the new business would bring. Carlson knew that, if pursued, this project would add considerably to the available hotel units in the core business area and would provide significant competition to the Multnomah in attracting large conventions.

Carlson also watched with concern the development of another project that would impact heavily on the Multnomah if it came to fruition: the establishment of a sports arena/convention center on the east side of the Willamette River just south of the Broadway Bridge. Spurred on by the growing interest in the city's near east side stimulated by the opening of Lloyd Center (Portland's first mall), the plan's backers were determined that building the Memorial Coliseum (as it was named) would add to the increasing commercial development in the area.

By the end of 1959 the project had received a go-ahead nod from the city and a schedule for construction had been drawn up. Catching the attention of the tourist industry, the pending construction of the Memorial Coliseum provided the perfect opportunity to establish motels and motor hotels, the new type of accommodation for automobile travelers wanting the convenience of on-site parking together with the luxuries of a hotel. By 1961, the Memorial Coliseum was drawing large crowds each week to sports and sales events like the home and boat shows, and the Sheraton chain had built a motor hotel a few blocks east of the coliseum adjacent to Lloyd Center. Before the year was out, another motor hotel, the Cosmopolitan, made its appearance a few blocks north of the coliseum. This addition of hundreds of new lodging units made a significant impact on Portland's hotel industry.

The Final Years

"Multnomah Hotel Up for Sale After 50 Memorable Years" read the headlines in *The Oregonian* on Tuesday, August 6, 1963. Blaming competition from newer hotels for a drop in its occupancy rate and resulting red-ink ledgers, Western had hoped to keep the hotel operating until it could be sold. With the financial condition worsening each month, Manager Bill Williams had had no doubt that it was only a matter of time before a deal was made and so announced that the hotel was on the block.

As it turned out, Williams' announcement was a bit premature, although not by much. The next day, Western issued a retraction, saying that the recent interest in the hotel by several groups was simply routine. But six weeks later, the inevitable occurred. On the fifteenth of October, Lutheran Homes and Hospitals Inc. announced it had purchased the historic hotel for two and a half million dollars.

The Lutherans planned to use the Multnomah as a "complete life care senior citizen center." They announced that modest renovations would result in approximately 400 "living units" being made available to retirement-aged individuals willing to spend anywhere from $2500 to $22,000 for a life lease. However, the sales campaign for Multnomah Manor was a resounding failure, and Lutheran Homes had to back out of their purchase efforts six months later. Immediately, Western announced that the hotel would continue full operation as a hotel and would resume making convention and tour group bookings. The "Grand Lady" had had a reprieve.

Alas, the reprieve was to be short-lived. The problems which led to the decision to sell in 1963 not only remained but worsened. Central among these was the increased competition from newer, more popularly located hotels. The near east-side continued to grow and prosper with the success of the Memorial Coliseum and the Lloyd Center, and the motor hotels in the vicinity were carried along in this success. Furthermore, the group planning to build a hotel just south of the Multnomah had finally struck a deal with Conrad Hilton, and the Portland Hilton hotel had opened in 1962. Forty years newer than the Multnomah, the Hilton then had the advantage of modern amenities, and a 12th-floor restaurant overlooking the city that drew dozens of locals and tourists eager to take in the spectacular view each night. By 1963, Portland contained more hotel and motel accommodations per capita than any city in the United States outside of New York, and the Multnomah's end was in sight.

The End

Sadly, Portland prepared to say good-by to its old friend, a friend who had embraced its citizens and reflected its triumphs for the past fifty-three years. Although most Portlanders simply recalled sweet memories of "The Grand Lady," others urged Western to consider alternative plans for the Multnomah's continued use. One such plan was explained by Regner W. Kulberg, MD, a permanent resident of the Multnomah who wanted to save his home. Hoping the hotel could be used as a place where "many older persons who want to live in the center of things could walk to work," he said:

> There [are] fifty or so of us who [are] living here and hope to continue to do so. We learn from one another that growing old is . . . something to look forward to, to plan for, to train for, to maintain health for. To be successful we feel that a senior colony should have a college for aging right on the premises, a training school in all the arts of growing old. The Multnomah has the room. The State Division of Continuing Education is thrilled with the idea of establishing such a school.

But, Dr. Kulberg was too late, his plan not feasible to those losing enormous amounts of money each month. Western announced that it had submitted a proposal to the federal Government Services Administration to lease the Multnomah as a government office building.

The end, when it came, came quickly. Just eight months after the Lutheran deal collapsed, Western was named low bidder on a proposal to lease the Multnomah to the government for office space. By July 1965, the Multnomah was to be ready for occupancy by the regional offices of the U.S. Forest Service and the Internal Revenue Service.

In four short months most of the loose ends had been tied up. The permanent residents found new homes; future reservations were transferred to the Benson, and inquiries about booking conventions were referred to Western's headquarters in Seattle. An auction of all the hotel's furnishings that were not going to other Western properties was scheduled for April 22.

The deep affection held by Portland for the Multnomah was apparent at the auction: thousands of people walked through the hotel etching its beauty into their senses and remembered the many milestones in their lives they had celebrated there. Literally everything that could be carried out was sold. One of the hotel's permanent residents, Leo Beckman, bought most of dishes, the stainless steel plate covers, the candle holders, and floor lamps. The dishes and plate covers eventually found their way to St. Vincent's Hospital. Another Portland restaurateur bought most of the Golden Knight's kitchen and serving equipment. Ray "Trader" Smith of Corvallis, owner of an appliance store, bought the Queen Marie suite and all the Pendleton woolen blankets decorated with the Multnomah's crest. Mr. Smith displayed the furniture in his store window to celebrate Mother's Day sales ("Make Your Mother 'Queen for a Day' With an Appliance from Trader Ray"), and although he tried to sell the set to Queen Marie's heirs, they turned down his offer. The French Provincial furniture remains in his family.

Many employees bought the beautiful mahogany desks, chairs and bedroom sets which by 1965 were 50 years old. Others decorated their homes with the elegantly framed prints from the Governor and Presidential suites. Even doors and mirrors were sold, as well as silver service pieces and a set of mounted moose antlers that had been stored for years in the basement. Finally, much to the amazement of even the auctioneers, the bellman's sink, used to clean any number of messy items guests brought into the hotel, dented and permanently stained with 53 years worth of grime, was bought by a woman who wanted a unique souvenir from the hotel!

After two days, the lower level and the guest rooms were empty and the final good-byes tearfully made. Many employees retired, many transferred to other Western properties, still others went to work for the Hilton or other Portland hotels. Men and equipment began to clear away walls, plumbing, and wiring in preparation for the standard-issue

Al Monner photo, Oregon Historical Society, Negative Number OrHi 72860

Renovation of the lobby in preparation for occupancy of the Multnomah Hotel by the government offices

government offices. "Drop ceilings, fluorescent lighting, new partitions, wall treatment, doors, and other detailing were installed throughout the building above the second floor. Major public spaces such as banquet and meeting rooms were turned into conference rooms." The Rose Bowl was closed. The lobby and the mezzanine remained relatively intact, but their former shops and service functions were replaced with modern glass and wood or metal storefronts. The Stirrup Room was allowed to remain open to cater to the public as always, and the exterior commercial spaces remained.

Over half a century of Portland's history ended in April 1965, belying the sense of rebirth and renewal that Spring usually brings. A piece of the city's heart was torn away the day the Multnomah Hotel closed, preventing succeeding generations of Portlanders and visitors from experiencing the pleasure that "The Grand Lady of Fourth Avenue" had provided to so many others.

Afterword

In 1995, spring came once more to the Multnomah Hotel, and Portland learned that it would soon resume its place as the city's best-loved hotel. After twenty-seven years of harboring the regional offices of the Internal Revenue Service and the U.S. Forest Service and almost four years standing empty, the "Grand Lady" had caught the eye of two local businessmen, Paul Christensen and Greg Daniels, of RealVest Inc., Vancouver, Washington. Businessmen unusual for their desire to stress the esthetic value of their properties, Christensen and Daniels were first captivated by the regal design of the Multnomah. A cursory investigation into the hotel's history further convinced them there could be nothing finer than to return to Portland that piece of its heart it had lost so many years before.

Inviting John Turner of Dimension Development Company, Shreveport, Louisiana, to join them, Christensen and Daniels found a hugely successful hotelier willing to share his thirty years' experience and expertise in building and operating hotels. The partners studied existing major hotel chains to determine which could best renew the Multnomah as a working hotel and restore its traditional philosophy of service, community involvement, and welcoming hospitality. They knew that the right group would enable them to restore the hotel to its former glory, allowing it to find its place once more in the heart of Portland.

After personally visiting dozens of hotels and interviewing their owners, the partners found a perfect match in the Embassy Suites. Having as its prime motivation the comfort of its guests, and its preference for a central atrium-like public space designed to draw its guests together in a warm and hospitable manner, the Embassy Suites continues the Multnomah's traditions, making use of the unique lobby and mezzanine and renewing its emphasis on fine dining and entertainment.

The grand opening of the Embassy Suites Downtown at the Multnomah Hotel was held November 15, 1997. More than two years had passed and millions of dollars spent to make over the drab office space into luxurious living suites. Once again, the Multnomah has a grand ballroom, junior ballrooms, and uniquely styled banquet rooms. The intricate lobby ceiling, first installed by Fred Shearer working for Tresholm Plastering, was restored by his great-grandson, Jeff, now president of Fred Shearer & Sons Inc., the family firm.

The lower level, once containing the hotel's storage rooms and maintenance systems, is now a health center with a swimming pool. Wonderful restaurants serve the finest in regional cuisine prepared in the hotel's state-of-the-art kitchens. Guests relax in the two hundred seventy-six suites, prepared with lavish care for their comfort. Bellmen park guests' cars once more at the Imperial Garage across Fourth Avenue from the hotel. As George "Bing" Sheldon, principal of SERA Architects in Portland, who oversaw the renovation, stated, "Our challenge [was] to give people a feeling of what was once one of the most elegant hotels in the city, if not the state."

To ensure the "Grand Lady" remains a part of Portland well into the twenty-first century, her exterior, lobby and mezzanine, as well as the Imperial Garage, have been placed on the National Register of Historic Places. Obliged to retain these areas in the same manner and for the same purpose for which they were originally designed, Embassy Suites has ensured that Portlanders will continue to cherish for many years to come the "Grand Lady of Fourth Avenue."

Courtesy RealVest, Inc., Vancouver, Washington

Paul Christensen, Greg Daniels and John Turner
on the mezzanine in the lobby of the newly remodeled Multnomah Hotel

Courtesy Pearson Air Museum, Vancouver, Washington

Tom Murphy and his Curtiss Pusher bi-plane getting ready on the roof of the Multnomah Hotel for the re-enactment of Silas Christofferson's flight of 1912

Airborne over Portland after lifting off over the northeast edge of the Multnomah Hotel's roof from the 200-foot plywood ramp

Courtesy Pearson Air Museum, Vancouver, Washington

Christofferson Redux

In summer 1995, although realizing it would take time for the Multnomah to attain its former glory as a working hotel, her new owners wanted to quickly bring back the "Grand Lady" to the people of Portland. The opening of Vancouver's Pearson Air Museum in September 1995 provided the perfect occasion.

To celebrate the air museum, as well as to let Portland know that the Multnomah soon would be opening its doors, Paul Christensen decided to re-enact Silas Christofferson's 1912 flight from the roof of the Multnomah Hotel to Pearson Air Field. In that year, "Goldie" Goldstein, the Multnomah's publicity director, had staged the original flight, the first between Portland and Vancouver across the Columbia River, as one of the hotel's first public relations events in June, four months after the hotel opened.

To re-enact the flight, Christensen went to John Donnelly, director of Pearson Air Museum. Donnelly found veteran pilot and aircraft restorer, Tom Murphy, and a replica of Christofferson's Curtiss Pusher in Hood River, Oregon. Thinking, "Why don't we do that again," Christensen set September 16, 1995, as the date for the re-enactment, and began tackling the mountain of paperwork that 1990s bureaucracy required. He asked the construction workers to

build a plywood ramp, two hundred feet in length, on the hotel's roof from which Murphy could take off. Christensen and Donnelly devised activities open to the public at both the Multnomah and Pearson Air Field to celebrate the September flight.

After several months of planning the logistics of the flight to accommodate the weather, the requirements of the Federal Aviation Administration, and the explosion of wires, television, and radio antennas that did not exist at the time of the 1912 flight, all was in readiness on Friday, September 15. With construction work already in progress, the interior of the hotel could not accommodate visitors for the flight, but carpeting was laid from the entrance to the one working elevator. On that carpet, thousands of Portlanders stood in line for over six hours to take a trip to the roof and marvel at the historic flight to come. After viewing the platform and the scene as Murphy would see it the next day, many of them hiked the few blocks north to Union Station to view the Curtiss Pusher and meet Tom Murphy as he supervised its preparation. With as much excitement as the crowds of 1912, the crowds of 1995 eagerly staked out the best location they could find to view the next day's flight.

Pilot Murphy, for his part, thought it was the most important flight of his career. On Saturday morning, a few moments before take off, he shook Paul Christensen's hand one last time and with tears streaming down his face, thanked him, saying, "This is the best thing that ever happened to me."

Despite earlier doubts, a few minutes before the scheduled 10 o'clock a.m. lift off, the weather improved enough to allow the FAA to give the go-ahead. To comply with safety regulations, Third Avenue was closed off for eight blocks north of the hotel and occupants of all the buildings surrounding the hotel were required to vacate them for the duration of the flight. Crowds in the thousands lined Fourth Avenue south of the hotel and on the roofs of selected buildings.

Murphy, dressed in a dark green, padded flight suit and old-fashioned soft helmet and goggles, climbed into the open cockpit, fastened his seatbelt, and revved the eighty-five horsepower engine to its maximum. Raising his hand, he signaled for the cable to be released, the Curtiss accelerated down the runway, and flew off the northeast edge of the roof. Although Murphy planned to lift off before reaching the end of the runway, the extra weight of the cameras positioned on the wings of the plane extended the take off run the full extent of the runway. Leaving the runway, he dropped about 15 feet before gaining altitude and heading north.

Accompanied by a National Geographic helicopter and others carrying local and national journalists, Murphy flew the Curtiss around building towers, power lines, and through clouds across the Columbia, approaching the river near the St. John's Bridge. Along with the flight enthusiasts in Portland, thousands watched on a big screen video at Pearson Field in Vancouver.

While Christofferson could never have fathomed the extent of the coverage (National Geographic aired a fifteen-minute video tape of the flight, and many news programs around the world showed clips of the flight for days afterward), one can imagine that Murphy's excitement at seeing the crowds waiting for him at Pearson was the same as Christofferson's, and that the landing he made was similar: "I came around the base leg and overshot the runway centerline a little bit, brought it back to centerline, and landed. It was a standard landing in a Curtiss Pusher, one bounce, two bounces, whatever."

The crowds at Pearson and in Portland celebrated Murphy's landing with loud cheers and broad smiles, just as they did for Christofferson eighty-three years before. Once again, the Multnomah was the catalyst for an event that captured the imagination of people everywhere, endearing herself to friends and strangers alike.

Murphy's flight was only the beginning of the Multnomah's renewed community involvement. In the spirit of Phil Gevurtz, Eric Hauser, and Eddie Carlson, John Steinbach, managing director, is determined to continue this same spirit of friendliness and hospitality always found at the Multnomah. Beginning with the November 15, 1997 grand opening, a benefit for the Oregon Symphony, Embassy Suites has set the path for the Multnomah Hotel to follow–to become known once more with affection in the hearts of Portlanders and people everywhere, as "The Grand Lady of Fourth Avenue."

Artist's renderings of the remodeled Multnomah Hotel lobby as designed by Peggy Dye, Corporate Furnishings, Inc. of Birmingham, Alabama, the skilled interior designer who designed the Multnomah Hotel for Embassy Suites. (1997)

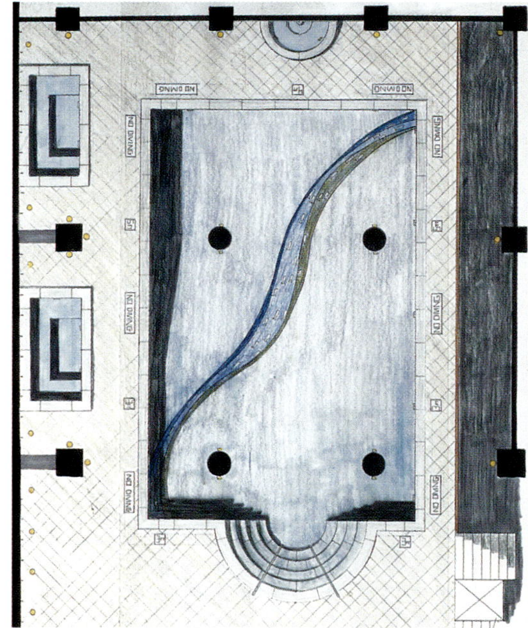

Artist's rendering of the pool design (1997)

Detail of tile work (1997)

A Note About the Author

Cáit Curtin was born in Portland, Oregon, graduated from the University of Portland in 1973, and received her MA from University College, Cork, Ireland, in 1976. In 1987 she founded CMC Research International, marketing and market research project consultants. She is Vice President for Business Development for The Kintock Group, Philadelphia, and divides her time between Philadelphia and Vancouver, Washington.

She is the author of "Doing Business in China, An Historical Perspective," *University of Portland Magazine*, Portland, OR, March 1987; "All-Ireland Cultural Society of Portland," in *Irish American Cultural Societies*, edited by James Funchion, Hoffstetter Press, 1983; and "Fred Bitte: A Seaman's Journey to Oregon," Oregon Historical Quarterly, Oregon Historical Society, Portland, Oregon, Spring 1980.

She has been a member of Phi Alpha Theta and has been listed in *Who's Who of American Women.*

Sources

The Oregonian and *The Oregon Journal*, Portland's daily newspapers. Coverage of the Multnomah Hotel was extensive in both papers beginning from its opening in 1912 to its close in 1965.

The Hotel News, a privately published daily broadsheet which provided travelers with descriptions of hotels and tourist information in the leading cities of the west coast.

The Columbian, Vancouver, Washington's evening daily newspaper, especially for its coverage of Tom Murphy's 1995 flight off the roof of the Multnomah Hotel.

Western Hotels Inc., corporate documents, board of directors' meeting minutes, and company prospectus.

Various Multnomah Hotel newsletters: "Multnomah Review," "Payday Press," and "Between the Floors."

Multnomah Hotel menus, brochures, and public relations materials contained in the Collections Library of the Oregon Historical Society.